There is no Software, ther

Digital Cultures Series

Edited by Armin Beverungen, Irina Kaldrack,
Martina Leeker, Sascha Simons, and Florian Sprenger

A book series of the *Digital Cultures Research Lab*

There is no Software, there are just Services

edited by

Irina Kaldrack and Martina Leeker

μ meson press

Bibliographical Information of the German National Library

The German National Library lists this publication in the Deutsche Nationalbibliografie (German National Bibliography); detailed bibliographic information is available online at http://dnb.d-nb.de.

Published 2015 by meson press, Hybrid Publishing Lab, Centre for Digital Cultures, Leuphana University of Lüneburg www.meson-press.com

Design concept: Torsten Köchlin, Silke Krieg
Cover Image: © Lily Wittenburg

The print edition of this book is printed by Lightning Source, Milton Keynes, United Kingdom.

ISBN (Print):   978-3-95796-055-9
ISBN (PDF):   978-3-95796-056-6
ISBN (EPUB): 978-3-95796-057-3
DOI: 10.14619/008

The digital edition of this publication can be downloaded freely at: www.meson-press.com.

This publication was funded by the "Niedersächsisches Vorab" program of the Volkswagen Foundation, by the Ministry for Science and Culture of Lower Saxony, and the EU major project Innovation Incubator Lüneburg.

Contents

TECHNOLOGY

PRACTICES

POLITICAL ECONOMY

INTERVENTIONS

DISCOURSE ANALYSIS

GOVERNMENTALITY

There is no Software, there are just Services: Introduction

Irina Kaldrack and Martina Leeker

Digital technologies permeate our daily lives. We access our social networks and the content we produce both individually and collaboratively, and other kinds of information from anywhere and everywhere. Along with the fusion of computers and telephones into smart, mobile devices, these practices are changing the concept and the materiality of software. In the past, shrink-wrapped software, as it was called, had to be purchased, installed on a *personal computer* (PC), configured, and updated regularly. Today, however, it suffices to log on to a single platform and install a *service* to easily access Dropbox, Facebook, Google, etc. In parallel to the development of *clouds*, web services, and mobile apps on the consumer market, "classic" software providers are moving to subscription models in ever-greater numbers: Adobe Creative Suite becomes Adobe Creative Cloud and Microsoft Word becomes Office 365. Software is no longer purchased, but rather can be rented. The world of PCs, in which hardware is embodied in an object and the *operating system* (OS) allows the user to install and execute software, is being transformed. The hardware is getting smaller and diversifying into netbooks, laptops, mobiles and tablets. The possibilities for their use—formerly provided by software in bundled applications and *graphical user interfaces* (GUI)—are now designed in cascades of services. The user's devices merely enable access to services that in turn, access spatially remote hardware and control processes.

This development within the consumer domain corresponds to a shift into *Software as a Service* (SaaS) for business. Accordingly, companies can lease IT-supported administration services for managing their employees, products, and customer data. Hence, hardware purchases are limited to Internet-enabled computers with access to a SaaS provider. There are no expenses to be paid in terms of servers or software, modifications or maintenance by in-house IT departments or external consultants. Instead, the company merely pays access fees. This saves companies money and time and allows them to concentrate on their core business, as the sales pitch goes, and to generate greater profits. Beyond that, promises are made regarding the services' ease-of-use, since these business processes like "product ordering," "delivery," or "payment receipt" are displayed and can be combined with relative ease. This means there is no longer the need to have expert knowledge of programming to optimise IT resources to one's own needs (see Neubert in this volume).

The publishers' thesis, "There is no software, there are just services," describes this situation as a radical break with the previous epoch: Hardware, once objectivized as a physical computer, is becoming distributed across different data centers and dissolving completely into infrastructures. And software, for its part, has to date, controlled the spacio-temporal materiality of hardware and offered up user interfaces, but it is dissolving in a cascade of services that organize access to data and its processing. Ownership of software is thus becoming obsolete, replacing goods as property through service use. This "use-economy" is open to all and promises empowerment: With these new services, everyone has the potential to offer their skills and goods for sale or exchange, as well as reinventing existing services through combination and modification. It is exactly this interplay between entrepreneurial services and the rising "participatory culture" that corresponds to a process in which any kind of aid or help, personal service or favor—our normal, everyday practices— can be subjected to the law of the economical (see Lison in this volume).

The thesis and title of this this volume refers not only to a situation of historical upheaval, but it may also be understood as a confrontation with a significant systematic argument of media science. The reference is of course Friedrich Kittler's claim that there is no software, but only hardware, because the technical operations occurring within the computers could be reduced to switches in the hardware, which are then merely made human readable by the software (1992). Lev Manovich provoked Kittler's thesis with the technical historical diagnosis, "There is only software" (2013, 147ff.), since all media forms, from photography to painting, have meanwhile dissolved into software in the age of digitalization. To describe the contemporary signature of digital cultures as cascades of queries and operations that are structured by bandwidth and connection speeds (see Parikka in this volume) is less of a reference to a historical upheaval à la Manovich (2013). As a variation of and commentary on Kittler's systematic argument, it is instead suggested here that there could very possibly be no such thing as stand-alone hardware either, because programs and hardware have always been linked as services (see Neubert in this volume). Following Thomas Haigh, one could go even further and say that hardware is part of a complex system, comprising programs, support, documentation, companies, distribution, engineers, and programmers, as well as learning processes and practices (2002, 2013). Hence, the following research hypothesis arises, referring to Kittler's systematic argument: Where hardware is part of a system in which "services"—in the sense of negotiating the use and commodification of distributable software among multiple actors—are crucial (Haigh 2013), it is not the technical conditions relating to hardware or software technologies that determine the situation, but rather politics and economies as well as practices and cooperative constellations (Erickson and Kelty in this volume; Gießmann and Schüttpelz 2015; Schmidt 2015).

The thesis, "There is no software, there are just services" is thus apodictic and inadmissibly simplified. Of course, there are products that are offered as software even in this age of services. Furthermore, it is yet to be seen whether a radical shift will take place from a software regime to the rule of services. But the pointed assertion is provocative in such a productive way that it practically forces the necessary detailed and sophisticated observation of contemporary developments in the context where services are ubiquitous, that it is likely to have a major stake in the configuration of digital cultures. With their contributions, the authors of this volume present this debate, which can be structured into the areas of *technology*, *practices,* and *economy.* Even if these different perspectives on services seem to overlap, each focus nevertheless yields specific results. In a history of technology informed by media and cultural studies, the interplay between software, services, and hardware becomes clear, quite contrary to the assertion that software does not (or no longer) exist (Neubert; Erickson and Kelty; Magee and Rossiter; Parikka). There have always been services, it is just that their use and emphasis has changed (Haigh 2002, 2013). The strong focus on practices (Fagerjord, Lison, Erickson and Kelty) as well as the economy (Lison, Magee and Rossiter, Parikka) each shows, in a different way, to what extent and with what consequences services as business models permeate other social domains. Thus, this publication takes up positions found in software studies that examine how different forms of software are embedded into the contemporary world. Herein lie issues of how software shapes subjectivities, commonalities, and working forms and how it is modified by them (e.g., the online journal *Computational Culture*; Fuller 2008 and Chun 2006, 2011). By focusing on services and with a differentiated discussion of the concept in the narrower as well as the figurative sense, this book provides initial orientation for researching services, as well as for effective interventions in a "services culture." The focus on interventions follows from the supposition that the shift toward services could lead to its own form of governmentality. This calls for further investigation and is yet to be explored as a level of critique of service cultures. With this in mind, each of the following illustrations of the individual areas implies particular options for intervention. This book aims to deal with the phenomenon and research field outlines above, but by no means claims to be exhaustive.

Technology

The contributions in this volume address the technological nature of services from a technical-historical viewpoint. From this perspective, the claim that an epochal upheaval is occurring in the transition from software to services invokes an immediate contradiction. As Christoph Neubert argues, what calls for investigation is in fact the relation between hardware, software, and services. This relation, namely, is negotiated anew for each specific historical point in time and against the backdrop of technological and economic developments. In this reconstruction, software appears to be an instable element that mediates between machine and business processes. The modularization and encapsulation of program functions and the blackboxing of those as services, interlocks technological continuities—from *object-oriented* to *agile programming*—with conceptual and discursive shifts. Seth Erickson and Christopher M. Kelty focus on this interlocking of change and stability. Their heuristic approach uses concepts from contemporary theory of evolution in order to identify "patterns of change and stasis, patterns that tend to preserve ancestry" (Erickson and Kelty, 42, quoting Wimsatt and Griesemer 2007, 283). Rather than insisting that abstract distinctions do exist between software and services, in the spirit of Bruno Latour, they ask in which "modes of existence" (2013) do different forms of software currently occur. Liam Magee and Ned Rossiter have selected the historical development of databases as a historical reference for their contribution. It becomes clear in their recreation, how technological innovation from *relational* and *non-relational databases* accompanies certain "politics of parameters," which in turn correspond to the policies of the organization and knowledge production, regulation, and control. Jussi Parikka takes his cue from Virilio (1999 [a], 1999 [b]) and looks at the disruption and collapse of services, namely through *denial-of-service* (DoS) attacks. In this way, he clearly demonstrates the technological conditions on which SaaS are based: bandwidths, transfer speeds, and the efficient management of traffic come to the fore and reveal how network policy application is involved.

These historical reconstructions point out the moments at which the technological conditions shape the transitions from software to services and their respective regimes. Thus, they signal possibilities for intervention within the interplay of technology, practices, political economy, and discursivations.

Practices

Services exhibit a two-fold relation to practices. First, the technological procedures within the service architectures dictate ways of programming as well as communicative and economic transactions. Thus, the use of files changes, according to Erickson and Kelty (49f.), through the use of apps: These do not just constitute the only access to one's own content in the cloud, they also fuse files to users, accounts, and platforms at the same time. Second, user practices have a reciprocative impact on the technology. Andrew Lison thus describes how the subscription model of Adobe's Creative Cloud makes the illegal cracking of licensed software, like Photoshop, practically impossible. This development seems to be a technical solution to prevent undesirable practices.

Anders Fagerjord shows how a differentiated picture of a technical culture of services can only be arrived at by looking at practices. He looks at the practices of app culture and exposes it as a part of services. The promise of the app industry that apps should be easy to program and use, as well as freely available, is quickly deconstructed, if one looks at the network of actors participating in app production. Contrary to the promises, a monopolization may be on the rise, as the economic policy of Apple demonstrates. These apps can only be programmed and used on Apple devices and are only available via the Apple App Store. Following actor-network theory (ANT), Fagerjord develops a model for analyzing how the combination of different actants and their interests can modify or even undermine the industry's service infrastructure.

Focusing on the practices shows that and how these are designed as operations and operation chains and can thus become trans-latable into services. By equating these, the productive moment in the interaction of a reciprocative influence of technology, economy, and practices disappears. This is what Lison and Fagerjord highlight to differentiate the software from the service culture. From Fagerjord's refined analysis, based on ANT methods and insights, one could deduce degrees of freedoms, which could help users to defend themselves against being forced into uni-formity inside the service regime and to interrupt the cascade of services.

Political Economy

If one focuses on the economic and social effects of the transition from software to services, the promises of companies operating these applications disintegrate rather quickly—promises like freedom and efficient time management. Rather, a new paradigm becomes clear, one that is revealed to be a regime of an all-encompassing service policy (Magee and Rossiter) and service economy (Lison). Markus Krajewski has made important preliminary contributions to our understanding of why and how technical structures and practices can turn into overarching regimes (2010, 2014). In relation to the question of whether a regime could form a service economy, Krajewski shows that applying metaphors is an integral component of the history of *distributed computing*—which is what the "service principle" referred to here, was called until the 1970s (2014). Metaphors like service, server, client-server architecture, or desktop, are used in information technology to make abstract technologies accessible, according to Krajewski. He points out that in the process, however, the metaphors unleash their own medial and culture-technical power such that technical, economic, and practical development gets promoted via the conceptual horizon of the metaphors in which these technologies are packaged. The metaphoric use of services is consequently not at all innocent but rather a constructive factor of service economies.

In their chapter, Magee and Rossiter point out that the orientation toward service above all entails a policy of control and regulation, which is not only focused on the organization of work but the whole environment itself, as the idea of smart cities demonstrates. The authors point out that since this regime of services goes hand in hand with the expansion of infrastructures that would style themselves as black boxes, it is difficult to arrive at a position outside the system. For Andrew Lison (67f.), services and infrastructures are becoming an ineluctable condition of existence in digital cultures, where they lead us hitherto unknown forms of work, remuneration, and ways of living. Such an example is the service, TaskRabbit, where highly qualified freelancers offer their services over platforms, either to their neighborhood or on the global market; from design through picking up groceries to babysitting. Business with services is quick, self-organizing, and purportedly both the freelancers and customers are happy with it. According to Lison, the problem with this, however, is that the differences between various professions and forms of work (immaterial, material, social-affective) are dissolving and being bundled into the radical economical impetus we euphemistically call the "exchange economy." Lison tells us this means neither goods, values, nor economic interpersonal relations exist in this regime, but rather only business exchanges that are no longer explicitly declared as such, and omnipresent, never-ending services. Drawing on Lison's argument, one could emphasize his diagnosis by saying both providers and customers become service slaves.

Regarding the issue of how the service regime could be inter-rupted, it becomes clear that attacks on services are not an option because they have long been integrated into the system. The denial-of-service attack is used by Jussi Parikka to demon-strate the technical foundations of service network politics, which comprise server capacity, the protocols of data traffic as well as bandwidths and the distribution of connection speeds. Parikka suggests that users of services relinquish control over their businesses, communication, and identities, and thus fall prey to the unstable infrastructural conditions distributing the services as well as being victims of the diplomacy of approvals and blockages of services instead of pursuing politically-grounded and legitimate regulation. Parikka hones his assessment of the consequences into the thesis: "There are no services, there are just vouchers" for access to services. He suggests that it is thus conceivable that a regime of services for services is being established in which access to the latter must first be enabled and secured via the former.

Areas of Interest for Interventions

In discussing the thesis "There is no software, there are just services," the economic perspective offers a less-than-encour-aging finding. Google and Salesforce.com partnered up in 2008 with the slogan: "Put your office into the cloud!" (Salesforce.com 2008). The aim was to create a profitable business model with apps and software for company collaboration—and it was to have been limited to this arena. However, this book claims that different service forms and technologies were indeed culminated into one service regime. This can be highlighted by posing the question: How can a business model and a corporate advertising slogan configure everyday digital matters as a regime of services and infrastructures, which furthermore gets promoted in self-organization, as demonstrated by activities performed by the mass of freelancers who are fixated on the sharing economy (see Lison)? In turn, both Neubert's and Erickson and Kelty's analyses, which are informed by media and cultural studies, show that one can only partially speak of a paradigmatic break with traditional software politics and the rise of a service regime. This insight can aid, i. e., in breaking through discursively-, economically-, and praxiologically-generated service logics. Even a look at the practices in the action field of services reveals a space for inter-ruption in the service regime where a pluralization of action instances can be described and thus suggests a relativation of the grand corporate promises of software as service (Fagerjord).

The broad and coarsely grained thesis therefore opens a productive tension for scientific analysis, one that unfurls between thinking through the consequences of service-techno-logics, and deconstructing service regime discourses and technologies. With this in mind, it is possible to develop methods for intervening in the services landscape, and to identify pos-sibilities for counteraction. Looking at the various aspects of services this way becomes necessary due to the signs that eco-nomic primacy is preparing to supersede the technical options as well as the practices that are not primarily economic and thereby to escalate into its own form of governmentality. The creation of such a governmentality may even be enabled by the users and constitute the services being conducted. The users may be invoking and organizing their own self-exploitation. All the while they are in control of their own self-determination and so-called participation as a policy of access to services at the technical and infrastructural levels.

Thank you to our colleagues on the editorial board, Marcus Burk- **19**
hardt and Andreas Kirchner from meson press, as well as our
research student, Leon Kaiser.

Bibliography

Chun, Wendy. 2006. *Control and Freedom: Power and Paranoia in the Age of Fiber Optics*. Cambridge, MA and London: MIT Press.

Chun, Wendy. 2011. *Programmed Visions: Software and Memory*. Cambridge, MA and London: MIT Press.

Computational Culture. A Journal of Software Studes. Accessed July 15, 2015. http://computationalculture.net/.

Fuller, Matthew. 2008. *Software Studies: A Lexicon*. Cambridge, MA and London: MIT Press.

Gießmann, Sebastian, and Erich Schüttpelz. 2015. „Medien der Kooperation. Überlegungen zum Forschungsstand." *Navigationen* 15 (1): 7–54.

Haigh, Thomas. "*Software in the 1960s as Concept, Service, and Product." IEEE Annals of the History of Computing* 24 (1): 5–13.

Haigh, Thomas. "Software and Souls. Programs and Packages." *Communications of the ACM* 56 (9): 31–34.

Kittler, Friedrich. 1992. "There is no Software." *Stanford Literature Review* 9 (1): 81–90.

Krajewski, Markus. 2010. *Der Diener. Mediengeschichte einer Figur zwischen König und Klient*. Frankfurt am Main: S. Fischer.

Krajewski, Markus. 2014. "Dienstleistungsagenturen. Zur Delegation von Handlungsmacht zwischen Subalternen und Software-Services." In: *Programm(e)*, edited by Dieter Mersch and Joachim Paech. Medienwissenschaftliche Symposien der DFG, 125–157. Zürich and Berlin: Diaphanes.

Latour, Bruno. 2013. *An Inquiry into Modes of Existence: An Anthropology of the Moderns*. Cambridge, MA: Harvard University Press.

Manovich, Lev. 2013. *Software Takes Command*. New York and London: Bloomsbury.

Salesforce.com. 2008. "Salesforce.com und Google erweitern Partnerschaft: Salesforce for Google Apps: Erste Anwendungssuite für komplettes "Office in the Cloud." Press release. http://www.salesforce.com/de/company/news-press/press-releases/2008/04/080414.jsp.

Schmidt, Kjeld. 2015. "Of Humble Origins: The Practice Roots of Interactive and Collaborative Computing." *Zeitschrift für Medienwissenschaft*. Web Specials. http://www.zfmedienwissenschaft.de/online/humble-origins.

Virilio, Paul. 1999. *Politics of the Very Worst*. New York: Semiotext(e).

Wimsatt, William C., and James R. Griesemer. 2007. "Reproducing Entrenchments to Scaffold Culture: The Central Role of Development in Cultural Evolution." In *Integrating Evolution and Development: From Theory to Practice*, edited by Roger Sansom and Robert N. Brandon, 227–323. Cambridge, MA: MIT Press.

SOFTWARE HISTORY

TIME-SHARING

UNBUNDLING

SERVICE-ORIENTED ARCHITECTURE

CLOUD COMPUTING

MEDIA ECOLOGY

AGILE PROGRAMMING

"The Tail on the Hardware Dog": Historical Articulations of Computing Machinery, Software, and Services

Christoph Neubert

The emergence of service-oriented business models in the computer industry over the last 15 years is part of broader historical dynamics underlying the relations between hardware, software, and services. This article traces the changing configurations of this triad with a particular focus on the economic, technological, and social construction of "software" in exemplary contexts. The historical evidence opens analytical and critical perspectives on the current rearticulation of software in terms of "services."

There is no software. It strikes one as a historical paradox that this claim, defended by Friedrich Kittler in the early 1990s with critical rigor against the ideology of human control over seemingly transparent computer hardware (Kittler 1992, 1993, 2014), resonates with business models hailed by today's computer industry under the labels of *Software as a Service* (SaaS) and *Service-oriented Architecture* (SOA). Taking this paradox seriously, I will consider the idea of an epochal transition from software to services pursued by the present volume under a broader historical perspective, starting with the observation that the distinction between hardware, software, and services does not lie in the nature of things, but is a product of complex historical processes. In essential respects, the current convergence of software and services reverses a historical development: The proposition that there is no software but only services describes a situation characteristic of the computer industry until the 1970s. The supposed decline of software has thus to be evaluated in the light of the emergence and transformation of "software" as technical artifact, economic good, and social dispositive. Witnessing its disappearance, the question arises: How did software come into being in the first place?

Systems and Programs

In the context of computing, the first usage of the term "software" in print is ascribed to the statistics professor John W. Tukey in 1958 (Shapiro 2000). The word was probably coined earlier verbally and in working papers, perhaps by Paul Niquette in the 1950s (Niquette 2006), or already in the late 1940s by the RAND mathematician Merrill Flood (Cerruzi 2003, 365, 372). However, according to the *Oxford English Dictionary*, the word "software" came into broader use not before the early 1960s, referring to the "body of system programs, including compilers and library routines, required for the operation of a particular computer and often provided by the manufacturer, as opposed to program material provided by a user for a specific task" (OED).

Cybermatics introduces "canned" software.

You buy it like you buy a can of soup. Software and hardware in one package, called the "Tin Can."

The soup in our Tin Can is a series of pre-cooked on-line software systems.

[Fig. 1] "Tin Canned Software" (Cybermatics 1971).

As this description already suggests, the historical notion of software crucially differs from our present understanding in several respects (cf. Haigh 2012). In a narrower sense, the concept comprised systems software such as operating systems, assembly systems, programming tools and compilers. In a wider sense, software was taken to include media such as punched cards and magnetic tapes, but also written documentation and even human activities such as system analysis or training. Being linked closely to computer hardware on the one side, and to all sorts of services on the other, software did not cover what we take as its essence today, namely applications. A second aspect distinguishing the historical from the present understanding is that software was not originally a commercial product: *Operating systems* (OS), utilities, and programming tools were provided free of charge by the hardware manufacturers, being considered part of general services a firm bought or rented together with a hardware installation. Programs for specific business tasks such as payroll, file systems, or accounting, on the other hand, were highly customized and usually written in-house by the data processing staff of the firms.

For a long time, software represented "only the tail on the hardware dog" (Bender 1968, 243). Accordingly, the software industry emerging since the mid-1960s was marginal and provided programming services rather than standardized products. Even where programs were offered as "canned" solutions (Figure 1), the proposed deal included hardware infrastructure, training, and customization. First attempts to acquire programs that had been developed by individual firms and sell them on a license-basis as packaged applications to other customers in the same business were not undertaken before the late 1960s, and with little success (Brown 2002; Head 2002). Even providing a catalogue of useful software solutions did not meet the customers' needs or expectations (Welke 2002). The idea to pay for software, especially for standardized products that were not even adapted to a firm's specific requirements, seemed to make no sense. The often cited "software crisis"of the 1960s manifested in scarcity of qualified personnel (Ensmenger 2010, 51ff.), but questions of structured product design and the Taylorization of coding labor in an emerging software industry did not become relevant before the 1970s. Indeed, the term *software engineering* in the sense of "the professional development, production, and management of system software" (OED) was first used in 1968 (Mahoney 2004).

Time Sharing

The bias towards services characteristic of the computing industry of the 1950s and 1960s was largely due to enormous hardware costs. Large mainframe and minicomputers represented expensive infrastructures that were supplied to customers in terms of a "computer utility rhetoric." Just as electricity consumers did not keep their own power plants, "it would be cheaper and more reliable for organizations to buy information processing from a service provider, rather than owning a

mainframe computer" (Campbell-Kelly and Garcia-Swartz 2007,
752). The technology underlying this service model is known as
time sharing. The concept of time sharing was developed in the
late 1950s, mainly motivated by the aim to make efficient use of
expensive mainframe computers by avoiding idle times. Time
sharing refers to the (seemingly) simultaneous access of multiple
users that are connected via terminals to a central computer,
technically based on the flexible allocation of CPU-time to con-
current user processes. The first experimental implementation,
the *Compatible Time Sharing System* (CTSS), was deployed at the
MIT in 1961 on an IBM 709 computer, followed in 1963 by the
CTSS II on an IBM 7094 that allowed access of 30 remote users
(Auerbach 1973, 65). Further time sharing systems were developed in the following years for various platforms by IBM, by Bolt,
Beranek, and Newman, and by General Electrics in cooperation
with Dartmouth College.

Evolved in universities and research centers, the technology
of time sharing translated readily into a business model. The
first commercial provider, Adams Associates, appeared in 1963,
followed by IBM in 1964 (Auerbach 1973, 65). Even with the advent
of IBM's System/360 in the same year, computing hardware
remained expensive and installations time and resource con-
suming, so only larger administrations and firms could afford
to rent or even buy the respective equipment and keep the
required personnel. Many smaller companies outsourced their
data processing activities and took recourse to the services of
time sharing providers, who offered remote access over public or
private data lines to computing infrastructure including hardware, programming environments (e.g. for COBOL, FORTRAN,
and BASIC), software packages, file storage, and print services.
Customers typically rented the required terminal equipment and
were charged for parameters such as CPU-time, connection time,
and storage volume.

Unbundling

The emancipation of a dedicated software industry from the previous economy of hardware and services involved two major steps. The first step was the emergence of the enterprise software sector since the 1970s, which was accompanied by a variety of technological, economic, and social innovations, including the standardization of products, new business and marketing models, a changing mentality of customers, professionalization of programmers, the rise of software engineering and corresponding methods such as structured programming and the systematic reuse of code in terms of software libraries, the development of interpreters and compilers for high-level computer languages, and the introduction of affordable and compatible hardware systems such as the IBM S/360 series (cf. Johnson 2002; Goetz 2002a, 2002b).

The efforts it took to invent software as an economic good and product in its own right is impressively illustrated by the incidents that led IBM to give up the practice of bundling programs with hardware and services. On January 17, 1969, the U.S. Department of Justice filed a suit against IBM, charging the company with monopolizing the general-purpose computer market; the bundling of services, software and machinery was taken to be anti-competitive and illegal. It took the Antitrust Division six years to bring the case to trial in 1975, and it lasted another six years before it was finally dropped in 1982, then considered to have been "without merit" (cf. Johnson 1982; Kirchner 1982). However, in preparation of one of the longest and costliest antitrust trials in history, some 30 billion pages of paperwork were provided. During the trial,

> Some 2,500 depositions were taken in all, and IBM compiled and stored in special warehouses 66 million pages of evidence. At the lawsuit's peak, more than 200 IBM lawyers were working on the case, on whom the company spent tens of millions of dollars annually. […] The parties called

974 witnesses [...] and produced 104,400 pages of testimony.
(Anthes 1989, 65)

While the case was negotiated, IBM issued internal directives suppressing the description of programs as products:

> We should realize that discussing [applications] programs
> separate from the machines in advertising or presentations
> is inconsistent with our fundamental position that hardware
> and software including programs are an indivisible product
> [...]. (cited in Arnst 1977, 4)

On the other hand, IBM reacted very fast to the legal issues raised by the Justice Department. An "unbundling task force" had already been formed in 1966 in the context of introducing the S/360 series (cf. Grad 2002; Humphrey 2002), and on June 23, 1969, IBM announced its decision to pursue separate pricing of hardware, software, and services. This date has been taken as the birth of the software industry or "Independence Day for software firms" (Gibson 1989, 6), though in retrospect, it is more likely that IBM's decision was not the cause but rather a symptom or effect of an emerging business sector. In any case, the unbundling affair provides a striking impression of the complexities raised by the emancipation of software.

Mass Markets and Pricing Models

After the quarrels in the enterprise sector during the 1960s and 1970s, the second major step towards software as a product is linked to the growing impact of the *personal computer* (PC) since the 1980s, which opened a mass market for consumer software (cf. Campbell-Kelly 2001). The PC served as host for packaged software applications offered to customers in *shrink-wrapped* boxes, and this software in turn played an important role for the domestication of computer hardware, its integration into the environments of offices and private households. At the same time, the concepts of *layered architecture* and *protocol stacks* as formulated in the OSI-reference model allowed to establish basic standards for the interconnection of computers, initiating the transition of the terminal-mainframe logic of enterprise computing towards the client-server logic of intranets and the Internet. Networked computing and the WWW opened new software markets for client and server operating systems (Novell Netware, Microsoft NT), web browsers (Netscape, Microsoft), web publishing software (Macromedia, Adobe), and antivirus software (Symantec).

The Internet business soon blurred the distinction between the economic sectors of services, enterprise software, and consumer software in the reverse order of their historical appearance: mass-market vendors such as Microsoft entered the enterprise software business, and later both consumer and enterprise software vendors turned to services (cf. Campbell-Kelly and Garcia-Swartz 2007, 736f.). The Internet also enabled new forms of collaborative work on programs leading to the *Open Source* movement. The impact of Open Source and "free" software, in particular of Linux, together with other trends such as the rise of mobile media and gadgets, the crash of the Internet economy around 2000, and the increasing commoditization of hardware and proprietary software led to the decline of the software product paradigm established in the 1980s and to new strategies of value generation. One interesting development in this context is the *appliances* model that returns to the idea of bundling proprietary software and hardware as a boxed product (Hein 2007). Appliances in this sense include consumer products such as game consoles, mp3-players, navigation devices, and personal gadgets of all sorts, but also enterprise appliances such as routers, or dedicated equipment for e-mail and firewall services. Another strategy employs marketing platforms for non-software products such as music downloads or e-books, the streaming of multimedia content, the promotion of social and business services, or the bundling of "free" software with advertising. These changes indicate a general turn of the computer industry

from vertical to horizontal integration and an orientation towards
downstream revenues and services. The remaining software
vendors were accordingly driven towards new pricing models:

> Traditional product sales and license fees have declined, and
> product company revenues have shifted to services such as
> annual maintenance payments that entitle users to patches,
> minor upgrades, and often technical support. (Cusumano
> 2008, 20).

Besides payment for maintenance, the classic one-time up-front
license fee has been replaced by subscription or pay-per-use
models that ensure a constant revenue stream, even during
economic downturns. Such pricing models have far reaching
consequences for the planning, versioning, and maintenance
of products (Olsen 2006). In particular, since the development
of new software releases and upgrades is mainly motivated by
marketing requirements "creating the illusion of a new product
to justify the repeated resale of what is fundamentally the
same good" (268), the subscription model eliminates the dis-
ruptive effects of release cycles. On the other hand, software
subscription tends to generate a lock-in of customers, which is
problematic especially for small firms and freelancers (see Leistert 2013 on the example of current policies adopted by Adobe).

Architecture of the Cloud

Quite different from promoting subscription under the guise of
a "service" is the idea to provide the functionality of software
applications in terms of web services: Instead of deploying a
copy of software to be installed and run on the customer's site,
the vendor hosts the software on his own servers and provides
access via the Internet. This business model is highly dependent
on technical factors such as network and server performance
and thus leads to the more recent paradigm of *cloud computing*.
According to the definition provided by the U.S. Department
of Commerce's National Institute of Standards and Technology

(NIST), cloud computing comprises three levels of services (Mell and Grance 2011): *Infrastructure as a Service* (IaaS) refers to the provision of computing resources (processing, storage, networks) that can be configured like on-site hardware and used by the customer to "run arbitrary software, which can include operating systems and applications" (3). The underlying virtual machinery is in turn running on a distributed cloud infrastructure with pooled resources. The model *Platform as a Service* (PaaS) refers to virtual development environments that already include operating systems together with "programming languages, libraries, services, and tools supported by the provider" (2f.). SaaS, finally, represents the highest integration level of cloud computing. The customer here uses the functionality of services without managing any infrastructure on the levels of operating systems, development environments, or application software (cf. Gajbhiye and Shrivastva 2014; Crago and Walters 2015).

Technically, the implementation of SaaS conforms to the framework of Service-oriented Architecture (Laplante, Zhang and Voas 2008). SOA extends the logic of *object-oriented programming* to commercial services, turning from algorithms and control structures to software components that are defined in terms of specific properties, functions, and interfaces; these components shall interact without central control in the context of distributed software systems. A web shop, for example, may invoke a number of services offered by different vendors, including database management, payment services, and logistical services, each in turn drawing on a number of subordinate services such as processing web forms, recommendation systems, or tracking options. These components are only loosely coupled, i.e. during an individual process, services are invoked on demand, their discovery, selection and binding being accomplished "on the fly" in a non-predictable way (cf. Turner, Budgen, and Brereton 2003; Gold et al. 2004). Activities in this context are no longer conceived as traditional programming; central process metaphors instead refer to aesthetic practices in the domains of music and dance—"composition," "choreography," and "orchestration."

In economic terms, SOA and SaaS neatly integrate with the management of business processes. The composition of services is accomplished by specific software tools such as the *Business Process Modeling Language* (BPML), an XML-based standard which is supposed to provide an efficient translation between economic and computational workflow. BPML was later succeeded by the *Business Process Execution Language for Web Services* (WS-BPEL), developed mainly by IBM and Microsoft and elevated to an industry standard by the OASIS consortium (Organization for the Advancement of Structured Information Standards) (cf. Turner, Budgen, and Brereton 2003; Candan et al. 2009). In this context, software has not only ceased to be a product, it also no longer represents a tool employed to accomplish specific business tasks: rather, both domains seem to converge in fulfillment of the old cybernetic dream that business itself becomes a matter of pure programming (i.e. music and dance).

Hidden Environments

The historical sketch provided so far might contribute to our understanding of the current service orientation in several ways: First of all, it becomes evident that the boundaries between hardware, software, and services, as well as the relations between the three domains, are fluid and subject to permanent historical change in conceptual, technological, and economic terms. Second, while hardware on the one hand and services on the other, fit into the classical definition of economic goods and represent fairly stable concepts, the status of software has always been problematic. Since its value depends on configuration, customization, maintenance, and training, software remains closely coupled to services. The emancipation of the shrink-wrapped box seems to represent a transitional phase, and even in the consumer market, complex and costly applications are replaced today by cheap apps that in many cases function as interfaces to remote services. Third, in economic terms, there is no clear-cut distinction between products and services, which rather represent the endpoints of a continuum. Different business models may rely on different strategies to "servitize" products or to "productize" services (Cusumano 2008, 26). Taken together, there seem to be no simple linear trends, but circular or other dynamics that govern the relations between hardware, software, and services, on micro- as well as on macroeconomic levels (cf. Cusumano 2003, 2008; Suarez, Cusumano, and Kahl 2013). Thus, the present boom of software and computer infrastructure as services can be regarded as a renaissance of essential aspects of the hardware and services computing economy of the 1950s and 1960s.

After all, there is no software. Kittler's speculative and hyperbolic dictum, formulated in the heyday of packaged bit boxes, was obviously inspired by personal experience with personal computers running Microsoft operating systems. But it was meant more generally, pointing to an inevitable strategic delusion rendering invisible the politics and power relations inscribed in hardware. Today, hardware and software retreat from the focus of "user experience" and are supposed to become part of the environment—the "cloud" as a kind of encompassing atmos-pheric metaphor, or smaller spheres such as the city, the home, clothes, or the human body. Before Mark Weiser formulated the agenda of *Ubiquitous Computing*, the late Marshall McLuhan emphasized the environmental logic of media, drawing on the example of the motor car. McLuhan claimed that the medium is not the vehicle, but the infrastructure, which he further described as a "hidden environment of services" (McLuhan 2005, 242). Thus from the beginning, the concept of "service" links the economy to an ecology of media—a managed ecology, however, of the cybernetic type, which is tuned towards operational closure and blackboxing. In particular, while software promises flexible control over hardware in terms of algorithms, services stand

for the possibility of flexible control over algorithms in terms
of functions. While software encapsulates hardware, services
encapsulate both hard- and software. In the era of services, both
hardware and software are running in *protected mode*.

Coding Services

So what are the real political and ecological conditions of infrastructures? What are the material and energetic resources of the
cloud, how are they managed, where, and by whom? How are
working conditions in software industries transformed by the
service paradigm? As a case in point, we might consider methods
such as *Extreme Programming* (XP) or *Agile Programming* (AP)
(Beck 1999; Beck et al. 2001) that are historically and system-
atically linked to SOA and cloud computing (Guha and Al-Dabass
2010; Baliyan and Kumar 2014). Following the requirement of
high responsiveness to changing demands, traditional development and production cycles are given up in favor of a general
acceleration of workflow. The "agile" paradigm departs from
central principles of structured programming and the factory
model of software production, considering thorough planning
and extensive documentation as harmful. The "Agile Manifesto"
and related commentaries (Beck et al. 2001) read as a peculiar
combination of working methods with moral values, yielding a
work ethic tuned towards efficiency, productivity, and customer
satisfaction. While emphasizing categories such as "individuality,"
"freedom," and "respect," many of the recommended principles
and methods are in fact reminiscent of the theory of "egoless
programming" formulated in the late 1960s by Gerald Weinberg
(Weinberg 1971, 47ff.; cf. Ensmenger 2010, 212–217).

For example, in smaller projects, all team members should be
present in the same room, maintain permanent communication,
and practice self-monitoring and mutual correction, which is
encouraged especially by pair programming in XP. Tasks and
roles are flexibly assigned and supposed to change, team

members are brought into direct contact with customers in order to react immediately to their feedback. Programmers are not rewarded for individual skills and competences, but for personal involvement. Work is accomplished by the team as a collective subject. Hierarchies are as flat as possible, central control should be avoided. Thus, in many respects, agile and related programs amount to a convergence of coding technologies and technologies of the self (cf. Neubert 2016). And obviously, the economic ideas of choreography, object-oriented programming, neat cycles, binding on the fly, and flexible work flow, return on the level of programming practices. Like other parts of the service infrastructure, human programmers belong to a pool of resources that are disposable and responsive on demand. In agile methods, the cloud becomes self-referential. Not by coincidence, *Human Capital Management* (HCM) is one of the most profitable services. While structured programming was linked to a Taylorization of software engineering (Mahoney 2004), "agile" programming and related approaches represent a next step towards neo-liberal, perhaps even post-liberal methods of coding subjects.

After all, there surely is a lot of software. So we might have to adjust Kittler's heuristics: *There are no services*.

Bibliography

Anthes, Gary H. 1989. "Rearview Mirror." *Computerworld,* March 2: 63–65.

Arnst, Catherine. 1977. "Bundled Pricing Illegal, 1968 IBM Memo Admits." *Computerworld* 11 (48), November 28: 1, 4.

Auerbach. 1973. *Auerbach Guide to Time Sharing*. Philadelphia, PA: Auerbach Publishers.

Baliyan, Niyati, and Sandeep Kumar. 2014: "Towards Software Engineering Paradigm for Software as a Service." *IC3, 2014 Seventh International Conference on Contemporary Computing (IC3)*: 329–333.

Beck, Kent. 1999. *Extreme Programming Explained: Embrace Change*. Reading, MA: Addison-Wesley.

Beck, Kent, Mike Beedle, Arie van Bennekum, Alistair Cockburn, Ward Cunningham, Martin Fowler, James Grenning, Jim Highsmith, Andrew Hunt, Ron Jeffries, Jon

Kern, Brian Marick, Robert C. Martin, Steve Mellor, Ken Schwaber, Jeff Sutherland,
and Dave Thomas. 2001. "Manifesto for Agile Software Development." *agileman-ifesto.org*. Accessed April 1, 2015. http://agilemanifesto.org/.

Bender, David. 1968. "Computer Programs: Should They Be Patentable?" *Columbia Law Review* 68 (2): 241–259.

Brown, Walter. 2002. "Founding Atlantic Software." *IEEE Annals of the History of Computing* 24 (1): 80–82.

Campbell-Kelly, Martin. 2001. "Not Only Microsoft: The Maturing of the Personal Computer Software Industry, 1982–1995." *The Business History Review* 75 (1) (*Computers and Communications Networks*): 103–145.

Campbell-Kelly, Martin, and Daniel D. Garcia-Swartz. 2007. "From Products to Services: The Software Industry in the Internet Era." *The Business History Review* 81 (4): 735–764.

Candan, K. Selcuk, Wen-Syan Li, Thomas Phan, and Minqi Zhou. 2009. "Frontiers in Information and Software as Services." *IEEE 29th International Conference on Data Engineering (ICDE)*: 1761–1768.

Ceruzzi, Paul E. 2003. *A History of Modern Computing*. 2nd Edition. Cambridge, MA; London: The MIT Press.

Crago, Stephen P., and John Paul Walters. 2015. "Heterogeneous Cloud Computing: The Way Forward." *Computer* 48 (1): 59–61.

Cusumano, Michael A. 2003. "Finding Your Balance in the Products and Services Debate." *Communications of the ACM* 46 (3): 15–17.

Cusumano, Michael A. 2008. "The Changing Software Business: Moving from Products to Services." *Computer* 41 (1): 20–27.

Cybermatics. 1971. "Tin Canned Software." Advertising. © Cybermatics Inc. *Computerworld* 5 (46), November 17, 1971: 39.

Ensmenger, Nathan. 2010. *The Computer Boys Take Over. Computers, Programmers, and the Politics of Technical Expertise*. Cambridge, MA; London: MIT Press.

Gajbhiye, Amit, and Krishna M. Shrivastva. 2014. "Cloud computing: Need, Enabling Technology, Architecture, Advantages and Challenges." *Confluence. The Next Generation Information Technology Summit. 5th International Conference 25-26 Sept. 2014*: 1–7.

Gibson, Stanley. 1989. "Software industry born with IBM's unbundling." *Computerworld* 23 (25), June 19: 6.

Goetz, Martin. 2002a. "Memoirs of a Software Pioneer: Part 1." *IEEE Annals of the History of Computing 24 (1)*: 43–56.

Goetz, Martin. 2002b. "Memoirs of a Software Pioneer: Part 2." *IEEE Annals of the History of Computing 24 (4)*: 14–31.

Gold, Nicolas, Andrew Mohan, Claire Knight, and Malcolm Munro. 2004. "Understanding Service-Oriented Software." *Software, IEEE* 21 (2): 71–77.

Grad, Burton. 2002. "A Personal Recollection: IBM's Unbundling of Software and Services." *IEEE Annals of the History of Computing* 24 (1): 64–71.

Guha, Radha, and David Al-Dabass. 2010. "Impact of Web 2.0 and Cloud Computing Platform on Software Engineering." *International Symposium on Electronic System Design ISDE 2010*: 213–218.

36 Haigh, Thomas. 2002. "Software in the 1960s as Concept, Service, and Product." *IEEE Annals of the History of Computing* 24 (1): 5–13.

Head, Robert V. 2002. "The travails of Software Resources." *IEEE Annals of the History of Computing* 24 (1): 82–85.

Hein, Bettina. 2007. *0+0=1: The Appliance Model of Selling Software Bundled with Hardware*. Master Thesis, Massachusetts Institute of Technology.

Humphrey, Watts S. 2002. "Software Unbundling: A Personal Perspective." *IEEE Annals of the History of Computing* 24 (1): 59–63.

Johnson, Bob. 1982. "Justice Department Decides IBM Case 'Without Merit'." *Computerworld* 26 (3), January 18: 1, 8.

Johnson, Luanne. 2002. "Creating the Software Industry: Recollections of Software Company Founders of the 1960s." *IEEE Annals of the History of Computing* 24 (1): 14–42.

Kirchner, Jake. 1982. "Bigness not Bad, Baxter Explains." *Computerworld* 26 (3), January 18: 1, 8.

Kittler, Friedrich. 1992. "There is no Software." *Stanford Literature Review* 9 (1): 81–90.

Kittler, Friedrich. 1993. "Es gibt keine Software." In *Writing/écriture/Schrift*, edited by Hans Ulrich Gumbrecht. München: Fink.

Kittler, Friedrich. 2014."Protected Mode." In Kittler, *The Truth of the Technological World: Essays on the Genealogy of Presence*. Translated by Erik Butler, 209–218. Stanford, CA: Stanford University Press.

Laplante, Phillip A., Jia Zhang, and Jeffrey Voas. 2008. "What's in a Name? Distinguishing between SaaS and SOA." *IT Professional* 10 (3): 46–50.

Leistert, Oliver. 2013. "Mietmodell Software Adobe." *Pop. Kultur & Kritik* 3: 39–42.

McLuhan, Marshall. 2005 [1974]. "Living at the Speed of Light." In *Marshall McLuhan. Understanding Me. Lectures and Interviews*, edited by Stephanie McLuhan and David Staines, 225–243. Cambridge, MA: MIT Press.

Mahoney, Michael Sean. 2004. "Finding a History for Software Engineering." *IEEE Annals of the History of Computing* 26 (1): 8–19.

Mell, Peter, and Timothy Grance. 2011. *The NIST Definition of Cloud Computing: Recommendations of the National Institute of Standards and Technology*. U.S. Department of Commerce. NIST Special Publication 800–145.

Neubert, Christoph. 2016. "Software/Architektur. Zum Design digitaler Dienstbarkeit." In *Dienstbarkeitsarchitekturen. Vom Service-Korridor zur Ambient Intelligence*, edited by Markus Krajewski. Tübingen: Wasmuth. (forthcoming)

Niquette, Paul. 2006. "Softword: Provenance for the Word Software." *niquette.com*. Accessed April 1, 2015. http://www.niquette.com/books/softword/tocsoft.html.

OED. S.v. "software, n." *Oxford English Dictionary Online*. http://www.oed.com/view/Entry/183938.

Olsen, Eric R. 2006. "Transitioning to Software as a Service: Realigning Software Engineering Practices with the New Business Model." *Service Operations and Logistics, and Informatics. SOLI '06. IEEE International Conference, 21-23 June 2006*: 266–271.

Shapiro, Fred A. 2000. "Origin of the Term Software: Evidence from the JSTOR Electronic Journal Archive." *IEEE Annals of the History of Computing* 22 (2): 69–71.

Suarez, Fernando F., Michael A. Cusumano, and Steven J. Kahl. 2013. "Services and the Business Models of Product Firms: An Empirical Analysis of the Software Industry." *Management Science* 59 (2): 420–435.

Turner, Mark, David Budgen, and Pearl Brereton. 2003. "Turning Software into a Service" *Computer* 36 (10): 38–44.

Weinberg, Gerald. 1971. *The Psychology of Computer Programming.* New York, NY: Van Nostrand Reinhold.

Welke, Lawrence. 2002. "Founding the ICP Directories." *IEEE Annals of the History of Computing* 24 (1): 85–89.

EVOLUTION

SOFTWARE

DURABILITY

MAINTENANCE

SCAFFOLDING

GENERATIVE ENTRENCHMENT

DEVELOPMENT

The Durability of Software

Seth Erickson and Christopher M. Kelty

Software is neither material nor immaterial but durable, entrenched and scaffolded. In this article we suggest that services and software should be understood through the diverse forms of durability and temporality they take. We borrow concepts from evolution and development, but with a critical eye towards the diagnosis of value(s) and the need for constant maintenance. We look at examples from diverse cases—infrastructural software, military software, operating systems and file systems.

A Software Coelacanth

In April 2014, a *60 Minutes* report made a brief splash when it
revealed that the United States live nuclear weapons arsenals
are using "antique" software and hardware, such as floppy disks,
microfiche and radiograph data and software written in the
1970s. The Internets mocked the hopelessly outdated technology;
John Oliver's studio audience for *Last Week Tonight* audibly gasped
when he showed them the image of a missileer holding an 8-inch
floppy disk. Oliver's commentary: "Holy Shit! Those things barely
look powerful enough to run *Oregon Trail*, much less earth-ending
weaponry."

Many people accustomed to constant updates, rapid release
cycles, beta-testing and automatic upgrades found the story
shocking—viscerally so since it concerns the deadliest weapons
on earth. The "silver lining," as a *Vice* article put it, quoting Major
General Jack Weinstein, was that "cyber engineers [who analyzed
the network last year] found out that the system is extremely
safe and extremely secure in the way it's developed" (Richmond
2014). The dramatic tension is thus driven by something unstated
(that newer technology is always safer, better, more efficient
than old, *legacy* systems) in conflict with something intuitive (that
it makes very good sense *not* to connect these weapons to the
Internet).

The software and hardware systems that run these 1970s era
Minuteman launch control systems are a kind of technological

coelacanth: a living fossil. Isolated, highly engineered, rigorously
(one hopes) maintained, but never upgraded or changed. Contrast this with what we might think of as the *cichlids* of contemporary software: mobile apps, games, websites, APIs and
services that appear hourly, where updates are constant and the
rate of extinction equally rapid.[1] The rise of *Software as a Service*
(SaaS), *Service-oriented Architecture* (SOA) or the *cloud* seems to
suggest that a qualitative shift towards a kind of hyper-insta-
bility is taking place: instead of a stable *program* nothing but a
temporary relationship of *queries* across interfaces and devices,
rendering something that was immaterial even more airy and
vaporous. It would seem to follow that our economy and culture
are also becoming similarly cloudy—precarious, uncertain, dis-
tant, contracted.

The apparent transition—from software to services—raises a
question: are they different? What is the difference, and how best
is that difference described? On the one hand, one might assert
that there is no difference at all because the concept of service
was built into software from the very beginning. Indeed, before
the word or the object *software* existed, there were *programming
services*.[2] Software had to be *unbundled* and *productized* to achieve
a stability and singularity we colloquially attribute to things
like Microsoft Word or Adobe Creative Suite. Whether it be the
computer utility of the 1960s or the *thin clients* and *netPCs* of the
1980s when Sun declared "the network is the computer," services
have been a constantly desired goal all along. On the other hand,
services today appear quite different: the ease of reconfiguration,
the openness of their accessibility, the standardization of their
functioning, and the reliance on a data-center-as-computer
model all seem to turn software, databases, archives, indeed

1   Cichlids are common, rapidly diversifying fish, comprising between 2000 and
      3000 species, including things like Angelfish and Tilapia, and exhibiting a
      stunning diversity in morphology and behavior.
2   On *software services* see Campbell-Kelly and Garcia-Swartz (2011), Campbell-
      Kelly (2009). Chun (2011) also makes this point.

even whole companies into ephemeral conduits of information, query or control. Stable productized software disappears in place of unstable, contractual arrangements—Adobe Creative Suite becomes Adobe Creative Cloud, Microsoft Word becomes Office 365—replete with a shift from a sense of ownership to one of servitude.

But the desire to fix the difference between the two falls into an ontological trap—demanding that the difference between the two be an abstract one of properties and kinds (and rights) rather than one of temporality and use amongst humans. Software studies occasionally suffers from a philological fantasy that the conditions of operation of software are territorialized by programmability, rather than the programmability of software being *terrorized* by time. Software and service are thus an entangled set of operations which are better viewed from the perspective of duration and temporality, and in particular that of an evolutionary frame, than from the perspective of code, conduit, circuit, network, or other aspects that privilege a spatiality or an intellectual abstraction that relies on spatiality to make sense of it.

So in between the coelacanth of the Minute-Man missile software, and the cichlids of the Apple App Store lies a whole range of software existing at different temporalities and with different levels of *durability.* An evolutionary approach makes sense here, but not simply in order to describe this diversification, but to critically analyze where and how value and values—novelty, most centrally, but also security, safety, freedom, health or risk—are structuring these temporalities. "Evolution is not just any change and stasis, but particular patterns of change and stasis, *patterns that tend to preserve ancestry*" (Wimsatt and Griesemer 2007, 283, emphasis added).

We are far from alone in turning to the ideas of evolution-both those who create software and those who study it frequently do so. For instance, within the field of software engineering, the language of software evolution often replaces that of repair and maintenance.[3] And so-called "artificial life" researchers have long fallen prey to the fantasy that because a program evolves it must be *alive* (Helmreich 1998; Riskin 2007). More recently, Lev Manovich, among others, has adopted a loose language of evolutionary theory—but only, he insists, *as a metaphor*—to explain change over time in the domain of media-production software (Manovich 2013).

Our exploration of evolutionary theory is not metaphorical, but critical and analytic, *viz.* how to analyze populations of software differentially, and in order to diagnose the values, ideologies or cultural technologies at work in and through software. Our focus is not on code or the program, but on the *population* of software—as engineers might say, the *installed base* of software, which necessarily implies an ecology of users, designers, maintainers, as well as organizations and physical facilities that must be kept running: made durable.

The durability of software is not an internal feature of a particular software program or service, nor a feature of an abstract programmability or mathematical facet, but instead a feature of its insertion into a social, economic and cultural field of intention and expectation where it *becomes* differently. The Minute-man silo stays stable for reasons that are different than the "stability" of the Linux kernel (which changes often, in the name of a stability that maintains an unknowable range of possible uses).

---

3   See for example the *Journal of Software Maintenance*, so called until 2001, when it was renamed the *Journal of Software Maintenance and Evolution*, until 2012, when it merged with *Software Process and Improvement* to become *The Journal of Software: Process and Evolution.* There are countless examples of the colloquial use of the term evolution in software engineering, but there are also more precise attempts to characterize software evolution, primarily as an analysis of the *internal* evolution, or ontogeny, of a program (facilitated by the technology of versioning control systems) such as Mens and Demeyer (2008). There is also a ubiquitous *phylogenetic* obsession amongst software programmers visible in the array of trees documenting the descent of different software, e.g. Lévénez's Unix chart (2015).

The becoming of a service such as Facebook Connect is much different than the simple query API provided by the *Oxford English Dictionary*. Both are services, both depend on money and humans who care about them—but the dynamics of their evolution and stasis are much different from each other.

Evolution therefore is not just a theory of change or duration—it is also about how aspects of the past are preserved differentially in different ecologies. Software does not evolve the same way everywhere—like life it is constantly *diversifying*. Recognizing variation, heterogeneity, and the preservation of the past in the present can serve an important analytical and critical function: to identify the values, ideologies and cultural technologies that keep some systems stable and slowly changing while demanding that others seem to change "at the speed of thought."

Software is not immaterial—this much is clear to anyone who studies it. But nor is software a *substance*. The replacement of software by services, if such a replacement is actually occurring, may be interpreted less as an ontological or material shift, and more as a shift in the relationships of concurrency, dependency and durability—software too has "modes of existence" (Latour 2013).

In this article we borrow two notions from developmental-evolutionary theory in order to think about the patterns of change and stasis in software: *generative entrenchment* and *scaffolding*. Wimsatt and Griesemer use these terms in order to argue for a *developmental* understanding of cultural and biological evolution, as opposed to a strictly gene/meme centered (á la Dawkins) one or a "dual-inheritance model" (Richerson and Boyd 2005). This is felicitous given the concrete fact that software is always paired with the word *development*—though we ought to be careful distinguish a "developmental biology of software" from *software development* as an established methodology. We argue here that durability—perhaps even "enduring ephemerality" as Chun (2011, 167–173) calls it—is a result of robustness and generative entrenchment—*viz.* when software becomes foundational or otherwise locked into a network of uses and expectations, signaled by *maintenance*—another key term in our analysis—and driven by particular cultural and economic value(s). Maintenance of software, as software professionals often recognize, is not quite the same as maintaining a bridge or freeway: it is not about wear and tear or the failure of particular bits of software. Rather it is about keeping software in synch with changes and dependencies made in other software and systems (Ensmenger 2014).

Layers, Stacks, Entrenchments, Scaffolds

In most engineering textbooks, information systems are *layered* into *stacks*—often a pyramid—with material, physical layers on the bottom and an increasing ephemerality as one ascends.[4] Such layers do exist, but they are hardly ever so clean. In fact, it can sometimes be harder, more expensive or more dangerous to change a bit of software than the hardware or the infra-structure on which it is supposedly layered or stacked. *Generative entrenchment* is a real feature of developmental entanglements, one that generates innovations by virtue of the very necessity of the entangled part or function.[5] How these entanglements came about is a not pre-ordained or mechanical: it is matter for historical research into the development of a project, the spread

---

4   There are numerous meanings of the term *stack* in the history of software. Sometimes it refers to an abstract data type in a programming language (adding something to a *memory stack*); sometimes it refers to a layering of different technological features, as in a *protocol stack*; and a more recent, more colloquial usage (e.g. *solution stack*) includes the range of tools—programming languages, package managers, database, libraries—that make up a particular web framework used for rapidly building and deploying apps in different contexts. What they share is the attempt to capture how software is always stacked, layered or interconnected in progress. No software is an island, etc.

5   Blanchette (2011) discusses the example of modularity's effects on *cross-layer innovation*.

of software, the standards guiding them (or failing to), and the reliance on expectations about the future of other components in a system, and the values organized in lines of force around a given software system.

Scaffolding as a concept serves a related analytical purpose. In building, scaffolding is necessary but ultimately disappears when a structure is complete (thought it often reappears for maintenance). In developmental psychology, scaffolding happens when people provide boundaries within which others can learn and develop skills. As they repeat these skills, the boundaries become less necessary. In the process of software testing, something similar happens: tools representing these boundaries (use cases, testing suites, different software environments like browsers, or common failure scenarios) are constructed around the software to test how it responds—as it is revised and improved these testing systems are torn down and disappear. As the software stabilizes and becomes more robust, it becomes generatively entrenched amongst other software systems and tools. Something of this process is captured by the process known ubiquitously in software engineering by the name of *bootstrapping*: the use of one software system to design or construct another that either supplements or replaces it. Similarly, beta testing might also be interpreted as using real users (or early adopters) as scaffolding.

The appeal to these developmental evolutionary concepts is not proposed simply in order to provide a description of pure dynamics, complex or simple. Rather, by identifying dynamics and patterns, we can show how the values and the logics operate: some entrenched software is maintained and some is not, and *maintenance* implies a set of *values* that require critical interpretation (Jackson 2014; Orr 1996). Not all software is maintained because it is *economically* valuable—Minuteman III missile systems, for instance, or the software that runs a power grid. Failing to maintain it may have economic effects, but it is maintained primarily in virtue of other values: security, safety,

health, mobility, secrecy, etc.[6] Even "archived" software must
be maintained, and represents particular values: preservation,
recovery, evidence (Kirschenbaum 2008).

Beyond Old and New

It should not come as a surprise that there is great diversity in the
world of software. What is surprising is that we have no good way
of taxonomizing it—or studying it—other than the language of
old, outdated, or obsolete vs. "cutting edge" or new. The language
of innovation privileges the linear and the incremental over the
spread of diversity or the interaction of different temporalities.
The supremacy of the value of novelty or innovation is a
peculiarly modernist and Western notion: novelty at all costs!
And it implies a similar and opposite mistake: to think of the old
as similarly linear and incremental—as deposited, archived, for-
gotten and in need of constant renewal. In fact, the perspective
of evolution demands a perception of newness everywhere
and in many different forms that persist: the past is not super-
seded, but preserved, differentially and in response to a changing
ecology (consisting of other things that are similarly new and old
at the same time).

The key critical or analytic moment therefore is not the
identification of the new, but the identification of a distinct
population—a kind of curatorial maneuver—the drawing of
boundaries around a set of instances of the same kind such that
diversity and differentiation are made to appear. A few examples
might indicate a different path for how to study software.

To begin with: particular populations of *operating systems* (OS) are
arguably the most entrenched—and most generative—aspect

6   In fact, there is a relatively robust economic niche where "obsolete"
     software is maintained, e.g. The Logical Company (2015) which re-creates
     "hardware, software and diagnostic compatible" versions of DEC's 1970s PDP
     computers, giving that software a new temporality and durability

of our software ecology. They come in many forms, from the consumer-focused iOS and Android mobile OS (which is on the order of 10 years old) to UNIX-derived operating systems (which are on the order of half a century old). Add to this the various populations that are in some ways both old and new. The OpenVMS and Alpha operating systems were originally designed in 1970s for DEC-VAX computers, but are still in use in old, new, updated, emulated and migrated forms; OpenVMS runs India Railways' reservation system and the Paris Metro's automated, driverless line 14.[7]

Similarly, entrenched programming languages (COBOL and FORTRAN) were at the heart of the Y2K hysteria. Although the predicted apocalypse did not come, it did reveal the problem of maintaining software—both its costs, and the kinds of values (in this case, fear of apocalypse) that are necessary to *disembed* entrenched software. Military systems, public infrastructure, factory process control (SCADA) systems, all contain various forms of entrenchments and dependencies—some of which are revealed dramatically (e.g. the case of the Stuxnet virus), some of which are revealed only slowly through maintenance or breakdown.

Entrenchment and scaffolding can also make sense of the variety of basic tools in use by software programmers—from compilers like gcc to programming languages, libraries and their bindings. The latter—language bindings—are a good example of generative entrenchment. Libraries of commonly used code in an operating system are often written in particular languages, such as C, C++ or assembly, often to facilitate re-use, and sometimes to make code more efficient (an algorithm in C can be made to run much faster than one in Perl, for instance). But because these libraries are "entrenched" in the operating system, they "generate" the need for bindings: bits of code that access and sometimes

7   See for example Hewlett-Packard Invent (2002) and Wikipedia contributors (2015).

recompile a library for use with another programming language.
Old technologies "scaffold" new ones: stories of programmers'
need to re-write a program in another language (whether for
efficiency or elegance, or to access parts of an entrenched
system) are everyday evidence of the scaffolding process.

Indeed, in 2015, the range of new programming languages
and frameworks for rapidly building and deploying software
have created vast but fragile webs of entrenchment and inter-
dependency. Web programming frameworks like Drupal and
Ruby on Rails are rapidly evolving—the underlying programming
languages (e.g., Ruby and php) are relatively new, the frameworks themselves are evolving as their developers refine their
approaches to the web, and (perhaps most importantly) the
individual modules and plugins for extending these frameworks
lead to a kind of "dependency hell." One commentator (Hartig
2014) reflecting on this historical difference in software said
"compiling a C program from more than 20 years ago is actually a
lot easier than getting a Rails app from last year to work," a clear
indication, as evolutionary theory predicts, that innovations are
abundant, but not necessarily advantageous.

Some kinds of software are *not* generatively entrenched, even if
they persist in time or remain durable. The Minuteman missile
base is an example—no other software or hardware depends on
the software created to control those missile launch facilities, but
it is nonetheless durably maintained as a closed system.

Other software is maintained *because* it is entrenched—both
technically and culturally. Take for instance the whole system
of software that makes an abstraction of a file possible: file
systems, memory allocation, attributes and permissions, and
directory hierarchies. As the authors of a Microsoft Technical
Report (Harper et al. 2011) point out, the concept of *file* as a unit
of data with associated attributes (e.g., ownership, permissions) and canonical actions (copy, edit, delete) has proven to be
remarkably robust, changing little over the last forty years. Most

operating systems are built around files, which manage allocation of memory and access to data; pipes and files were central to the design of UNIX, which treats *everything* as a file, including external devices like printers (accessed through *device files*). Humans are also built around files: we expect them to function in particular ways, to be stable and findable, to be *ownable* and *sharable.*

Although the file is a seemingly essential concept, it is challenged by *service oriented computing* or *cloud computing* where a new kind of "social" data is associated with files, and where files exist simultaneously on multiple devices. In this case it is not so much a particular piece of software code, but an essential "abstraction" (and an implied set of interoperable components) that is entrenched both in the hardware, and in the expectations of users. It is generative because the file cannot simply be replaced *in toto,* but rather must be "piecewise" re-engineered, guided by particular values.

Blanchette's example (2011) of the Google File System demonstrates that even if the file is not what it used to be, we still need the abstraction as a way to get the file to appear manipulable and stable on a set of virtualized servers (preserving it, and further entrenching it). Engineers might agree that there are "better" ways to do things, but the file cannot be so easily disembedded from both human and machine consciousness.

But: *it is changing.* Scaffolding can help us see how. iOS and Android operating systems both "hide" files from users. They are not yet gone—the OS still relies on them—but are embedded inside an app which has very quickly become the primary mode of interacting with software on most devices (Apple 2014). It is very hard to "open a file" on a phone or iPad, because the system is designed to hide files and metadata about files inside an app—which is now intended to be the primary abstraction for humans. For most purposes, however, apps do not require users to open or close important files, and they solve the question of "where is my stuff?" by putting it inside the app (and "in the cloud"). This creates a kind of scaffold whereby users can change from an understanding of apps that open files, to one where apps have data and resources tied to users, accounts and devices. Some populations change faster than others.

This transition, however, is not simply an evolutionary fact. Rather, by understanding the generative entrenchment and scaffolding of files and apps, we can turn a more critical eye on what are otherwise simply dubbed technological or engineering concerns. Among other things, the file abstraction supports a particular model of property rights in which digital objects are literally designed around stable property ownership: files must have owners and permissions. Apps, by contrast, are designed around a different field of rights and laws: contracts and terms of service—specifically non-negotiable contracts in which the app provider has significantly more rights than the app user.

This is the "cultural technique" at the heart of the transition from software to services: 20th century intellectual property rights law was designed for intangible property fixed in "tangible media" and the myriad ways in which media was so fixed in the era of *Film, Gramophone, Typewriter* (Kittler 2006). Contract law, by contrast is not about a relationship between the intangible and the tangible, it is about the fixed duration of a relationship of trust, and a way of structuring the future in terms of liability and responsibility. It is not an either/or situation, but as more and more users enter into contracts, instead of purchasing property, the software itself changes to support this cultural practice.

Apodosis: Legacy

The word *legacy* is one with a precise meaning in the history of information technology. Legacy systems are every IT manager's bogeyman; they are the cause of *lock-in* they are the emblem of the evils of *proprietary* software; they are the cause of Y2K bugs and the scourge of cyber-security, they represent the evils of corporate capitalism, the domination against which *free* software and *Open Source* are often pitched in battle.

But if evolution is "particular patterns of change and stasis *that preserve ancestry*" then there is no way out of a legacy. Not all legacies are equally momentous, however, just as not all inheritances are equally large. We would do well to develop a better understanding of how ancestry has been and is preserved in software systems, if we want to make any claim that innovations like SaaS actually represent some break with the past. On the contrary—some services will become entrenched; the seemingly flexible solution stack of today is the legacy system of tomorrow. Even more importantly, there is no single legacy, but a pattern of differences: a diversification with respect to environment. And if we want to analyze the difference these differences make, we must move away from treating software as substance—whether material substance or thought substance: program, code, algorithm.

Actor Network Theory makes a simple point here: we do not live in a world with humans as the foundation, nor in one simply run by the automaticities of machines, but in a world of relations and modes. The difference that software makes depends on how it is inserted into the relations amongst our associations—but it is not inserted the same way everywhere. The effect of software—the difference it makes—depends on the "patterns of change and stasis which preserve ancestry" at play in any given case.

Thinking in terms of scaffolding and generative entrenchment might be an antidote to the relentless anti-humanist teleology so common in both popular and scholarly thinking. That teleology—a kind of neo-Spencerianism—is driven by punditry and criticism that demands of software (and technology generally) that it obey a law of ever-complexifying, ever-accelerating progress towards either the domination of some imagined all-powerful capitalism or the liberation-destruction

of some fantasized autonomous artificial intelligence.[8] This
Refrain of Constantly Accelerating Change contains a grain of
truth—software has enabled new patterns, new durabilities—but
it misses the *existence* of diversity in the world, and the ways in
which it preserves ancestry. To view software evolution as an
institutionally and culturally heterogeneous object might allow us
to critically diagnose its real effects, rather than running ahead to
the next new thing in order to declare its sudden dominance, and
the irrelevance of all the rest.

*We thank the Part.Public.Part.Lab members for valuable con-
versation and feedback, Irina Kaldrack and Martina Leeker for
incisive comments, and the Digital Cultures Research Lab of Leuphana University for the invitation to contribute*

Bibliography

Apple. 2014. "File System Basics." *iOS Developer Library*. Accessed May 23, 2015.
   https://developer.apple.com/library/ios/documentation/FileManagement/Con-
   ceptual/File SystemProgrammingGuide/FileSystemOverview/FileSystemOver-
   view.html.
Blanchette, Jean-François. 2011. "A Material History of Bits." *Journal of the American
   Society for Information Science and Technology* 62 (6): 1042–1057.
Bogost, Ian. 2015. "The Cathedral of Computing." *Atlantic Monthly*, January 15.
   Accessed May 25, 2015. http://www.theatlantic.com/technology/archive/2015/01/
   the-cathedral-ofcomputation/384300/.
Campbell-Kelly, Martin. 2009. "Historical reflections: The Rise, Fall, and Resurrection
   of Software as a Service." *Communications of the ACM* 52 (5): 28.
Campbell-Kelly, Martin, and Daniel D. Garcia-Swartz. 2011. "From Products to
   Services: The Software Industry in the Internet Era." *Business History Review* 81
   (4): 735–764.
Chun, Wendy. 2011. *Programmed Visions: Software and Memory*. Cambridge, MA: MIT
   Press.

8   See, for example, Ian Bogost's op-ed on the subject "The Cathedral of
     Computation" (2015).

54   Ensmenger, Nathan. 2014. "When Good Software Goes Bad: The Surprising Durability of an Ephemeral Technology." In *MICE (Mistakes, Ignorance, Contingency, and Error) Conference.* Munich. Accessed May 23, 2015. http://homes. soic.indiana.edu/nensmeng//files/ensmenger-mice.pdf.

Harper, Richard, Eno Thereska, Siân Lindly, Richard Banks, Phil Gosset, William Odom, Gavin Smith, and Eryn Whitworth. 2011. *What Is a File? Microsoft Research Technical Report MSR-TR-2011-109.* Redmond, WA.

Hartig, Pascal. 2014. "Building Vim from 1993 Today." *SVBTLE.* Accessed May 23, 2015. http://passy.svbtle.com/building-vim-from-1993-today.

Helmreich, S. 1998. "Recombination, Rationality, Reductionism and Romantic Reactions: Culture, Computers, and the Genetic Algorithm." *Social Studies of Science* 28 (1): 39–71.

Hewlett-Packard Invent. 2002. "Success Story." Accessed May 25, 2015. http://h71000.www7.hp.com/openvms/brochures/indiarr/.

Jackson, Steven J. 2014. "Rethinking Repair." In *Media Technologies: Essays on Communication, Materiality and Society*, edited by Tarleton Gillespie, Pablo J. Boczkowski, and Kirsten A. Foot: 221–239. Cambridge, MA: MIT Press.

Kirschenbaum, Matthew. 2008. *Mechanisms: New Media and the Forensic Imagination.* Cambridge, MA: MIT Press.

Kittler, Friedrich A. 2006. *Gramophone, Film, Typewriter.* Stanford, CA: Stanford University Press.

Latour, Bruno. 2013. *An Inquiry into Modes of Existence: An Anthropology of the Moderns.* Cambridge, MA: Harvard University Press.

Lévénez, Eric. 2015. "Unix History." Accessed May 23, 2015. http://www.levenez.com/unix/.

Manovich, Lev. 2013. *Software Takes Command: Extending the Language of New Media.* London: Bloomsbury Publishing.

Mens, Tom, and Serge Demeyer. 2008. *Software Evolution.* New York, NY; London: Springer.

Nato. 1968. "Software Engineering." Report on a conference sponsored by the *NATO SCIENCE COMMITTEE.* October 7–11, Garmisch. Accessed May 27, 2015. http://homepages.cs.ncl.ac.uk/brian.randell/NATO/nato1968.PDF.

Orr, Julian E. 1996. *Talking About Machines: An Ethnography of a Modern Job.* Ithaca, NY: ILR Press/Cornell University Press.

Richerson, Peter J., and Robert Boyd. 2005. *Not by Genes Alone: How Culture Transformed Human Evolution.* Chicago, IL: University of Chicago Press.

Richmond, Ben.2014 "America's Nuclear Arsenal Still Runs Off Floppy Disks." *Motherboard (Vice Magazine)*, April. Accessed May 23, 2015. http://motherboard.vice.com/read/americas-nuclear-arsenal-still-runs-off-floppy-disks.

Riskin, Jessica. 2007. *Genesis Redux: Essays in the History and Philosophy of Artificial Life.* Chicago, IL: University of Chicago Press.

The Logical Company. 2015. "Home." Accessed May 23, 2015. http://www.logical-co.com/.

Wikipedia contributors. 2015 "Paris Métro Line 14." *Wikipedia: The Free Encyclopedia*. Last modified May 24, 01:58 CET. Accessed May 25, 2015. http://en.wikipedia.org/wiki/Paris_M%C3%A9tro_Line_14.

Wimsatt, William C., and James R. Griesemer. 2007. "Reproducing Entrenchments to Scaffold Culture: The Central Role of Development in Cultural Evolution." In *Integrating Evolution and Development: From Theory to Practice*, edited by Roger Sansom and Robert N. Brandon, 227–323. Cambridge, MA: MIT Press.

SHRINK-WRAP SOFTWARE

MULTIMEDIA

DIGITAL MEDIA

SERVICE ECONOMY

COMMODITY CULTURE

From Shrink Wrap to Services: The Universal Machine and Universal Exchange

Andrew Lison

The shift within digital media from software to services represents a level of ubiquity above and beyond that of multimedia, the digital's relation of previously-existing forms of media within its binary system of equivalence, and into the relation of social relations themselves. In this sense, it both mirrors and complements the global spread of capitalism, which also seeks to make both goods and relations equivalent (but not equal) through the money form. Tracing this shift, this chapter examines connections between the development of end-user Software as a Service and the service economy enabled by mobile apps like Uber and TaskRabbit to argue that "service" in this context should be understood as the universal medium's extraction of value from the increasingly universalized process of exchange.

Information is the key commodity in the
organizational logic of protocological control.
(Galloway and Thacker 2007, 57)

The digital is a totalizing force. The history of its development
as medium, which is equally the history of its development as
concept, is the progressive subsumption of previously existing
methods, media, and, eventually, relations into fundamentally
binary logics of (re)production and transmission. Thus, when
Friedrich Kittler asserts that "There is no Software," he does so
in order to highlight the capabilities (and, ultimately, limitations)
of Turing's *universal machine*, wherein the potential for this subsumption resides, as opposed to any individual program, which
can only represent a particular instance of it (Kittler 1995). Capital, too, effects a similar totalization, rendering human relations
as much as the goods they produce comprehensible through
a logic of universal exchange, one that simultaneously and
paradoxically implies both equality (all social transactions can be
made equivalent, for they can be effected by conversion into the
money form) and inequality (one side of the transaction—that of
the capitalist—nevertheless accrues more value than the other).
If software is the mechanism by which specific processes and
media become interchangeable aspects of the universal machine,
then globalization is the process by which individual regions,
peoples, and labor practices are incorporated within a worldwide
system of capitalist political economy. Thus, significant work considering the encounter between a globalizing capitalist tendency
and regional particularity notwithstanding (e.g. Tsing 2005),
analyses of capitalism as a totalizing force remain key to fully
accounting for both its power and drive.

The question thus arises of the relation between the digital and
global or late capitalism, as Marxist thinkers have often termed
it (e.g. Mandel 1978, Jameson 1991). It has been a foundational

tenet of Marxist epistemology that, contrary to the way I
have described it above, universal exchange has served to
obscure human relations rather than—or, to be more precise,
simultaneously instead of and in addition to—rendering them
into a system of equivalence. Thus, the critique of the commodity
form laid out in the opening of *Capital* and, hence, the many subsequent attempts to lift, provisionally and in advance of a really-
existing communist society, the "veil...from the countenance
of the social life-process" (Marx 1976, 173) by way of demys-
tificatory analysis and, subsequently, avant-garde *Verfremdung*,
the latter being the very technique that, as Lev Manovich has
argued, graphical digital interfaces ultimately defang by fully
incorporating (Manovich 2001, 306–307). Yet the rise of *graphical
user interfaces* (GUI) in the late 1980s and early 1990s, and especially the multimedia software that accompanied them, situates
software at a paradoxical nexus in that the critique it renders
toothless is outlasted by the very form it was meant to critique.
This form is not so much capitalism itself as it is its specifically
commoditized manifestation, which reaches its apotheosis in the
shrink-wrapped software package and, in doing so, also outlasts—
if only just barely—the really-existing "communist" societies of
Eastern Europe.

To say that the commodity peaks with the advent of the shrink-
wrapped software package is not to say that shrink-wrapped
software somehow represents the ideal, Platonic commodity.
Rather, it is to assert that shrink-wrapped software indicates
the final moments of a political economy fundamentally predicated upon the commodity form, that is, one in which nearly all
socio-economic relations, even those primarily effected through
medium-agnostic "informational" products, are masked through
the circulation of material goods. The view of modern media
as essentially a function of technological reproducibility has
been in play at least since Walter Benjamin's analysis (Benjamin
1968), if not the advent of movable type itself, but the anti-
nomies between a commodity in which a fixed amount of labor

is invested and one in which an initial, extensive outlay of labor is subsequently amortized over large numbers of comparatively inexpensive copies is stretched to its breaking point in shrink-wrapped multimedia software.[1] At the root of these contradictions lies the question of whether consumers are purchasing an object to do with as they please (including copying whatever content it may contain), or a license to the content contained *within* the object, to which they are subsequently subject to restrictions.[2] The question of licensing becomes crucial precisely at the moment that media are no longer confined to the objects in which the industrial production process has enshrined them but become effortlessly reproducible, which is to say subject to piracy (Kittler 1995). Already the lesson of 1980s campaigns like the British Phonographic Industry's (BPI) "Home Taping is Killing Music," in the case of digital multimedia so-called intellectual commodities become reproducible without so much as the degradation of quality induced by analog reproduction. Consequently, the BPI campaign was followed shortly thereafter by both a cavalcade of digitally-enabled sampladelia in the popular music of the late 1980s and a renewed focus on copyright law within the industry (see, for example, Clover 2009, 25–50). Shrink-wrapped software represents the apotheosis of the commodity form because, without the deliberate addition of

1   This problematic is not easily reducible to the classical Marxist distinction between fixed and variable capital in that components of the culture/media industry's creative process, in pre-networked times, were (and still often are) generally not themselves able to be commoditized as easily (if at all) as its output was. Thus, "creative" costs (storytellers, directors, musicians, programmers, etc.) remain to a large extent variable; one cannot (yet?) purchase a scripting machine at fixed cost and thereby make professional screenwriters obsolete, although one *can* now "crowdsource" them.

2   It is of course imperative to consider this question in relation to the music industry's own shift to digital media with the compact disc in the early 1980s, a shift predicated upon convincing consumers to repurchase their favorite recordings as new media commodities and most decidedly not characterized in terms of any kind of "media upgrade license" affording those who already owned them on vinyl or cassette the right to experience them on a new format. See also Sterne (2012), 219.

"copy protection," it is the first commodity that can be exactingly
yet painlessly copied by end-users on a massive scale and thus,
in a sense, the last. This is a problem analyzed by Kittler from
the perspective of what might still barely be called production,
or *software development*: the impossibility of claiming ownership
of a universally computable algorithm that must be overcome in
order to ground the rise of software as commodity (Kittler 1995).[3]
On the side of what might equally as tenuously still be described
as consumption, that of the end-user, consider instead in this
regard The Software Publishers Association's (SPA) infamous
1992 "Don't Copy That Floppy" video, which tellingly highlights

3   For Kittler, software compilation enables universally computable algorithms
to become obscured and thus property, a process which he productively
but erroneously equates with mathematical encryption: "The ever-growing
hierarchy of high-level programming languages works exactly the same
way as one-way functions in recent mathematical cryptography...For
software, this cryptographic effect offers a convenient way to bypass
the fact that by virtue of Turing's proof the concept of mental property
as applied to algorithms has become meaningless...Every license, every
dongle, every trademark...prove[s] the functionality of one-way functions"
(Kittler 1995). In actuality, the distinction between the two is key: decoding
a message encrypted with a sufficiently advanced "one-way" algorithm,
while so computationally intensive as to remain infeasible without the
key with which it has been encrypted, nevertheless produces an exact
replica of the encoded message when performed successfully; there is no
such guarantee with decompilation. Although crucial for the reification of
software into a commodity, compilation might be more accurately anal-
ogized to a kind of lossy compression. To put it another way, decompilation
is properly undecidable, with only a partial reconstruction existing in the
complexity class NP-complete (Horspool and Marovac 1980, 223, 227), while
by contrast full decryption of a "one-way" ciphertext without the key is,
at best, as Kittler describes, NP-complete. (What Claude Shannon defines
as a "Perfect Secrecy" system, however, would be properly undecidable
because the number of possible decryptions would equal the number of
possible plaintext messages (Shannon 1949, 659). Such a system carries
the difficult requirement of a truly random key, pre-shared between the
sender and receiver, of equal or greater informational value (e.g., length)
to the message to be encrypted; contemporary digital encryption systems
generally trade this undecidable perfection for smaller amounts of entropy
(i.e., manageable key length), reusability, and the possibility of public, yet
reasonably secure, key exchange).

the issue of software piracy through a musical form then at the height of its popularity, hip-hop.

The video begins with two schoolchildren debating whether to copy a game in order to take it home and continue playing when "DP," a rapping "disk protector," appears on their computer screen to discourage them. Citing the economic costs of copying software, DP, played by actor and lawyer M.E. Hart, explicitly connects the software industry to the retail store:

> One leads to another then ten then more
> and no one buys any disks from the store
> so no one gets paid and they can't make more
> the posse breaks up and that closes the stores.
> (SPA/M.E. Hart 1992)

Indeed, the video seems to suggest that software is inseparable from the physical medium in which it is inscribed:

> The more you take the less there will be
> the disks become fewer, the games fall away
> the screen starts to shrink and then it will fade
> programs fall through a black hole in space
> the computer world becomes bleak and stark
> loses its life and the screen goes dark.
>
> Welcome to the end of the computer age.
> (SPA/M.E. Hart 1992)

The "computer age" here is unthinkable not simply without a material support (an observation unremarkable to the point of obviousness) but without a very specific material support, the floppy disk, and the system of economic relations—again not simply capitalism but a specific system of commodity distribution and retail sales—that enables it. Yet the video itself not only seems aware of the uphill battle it faces in convincing computer-savvy kids not to pirate software (at one point it even seemingly admits that it is often trivial to do so), it relies on the very features of iterability whose deployment it seeks to curtail in its audience.

Hip-hop, of course, as Joshua Clover has noted, is perhaps the popular musical genre most closely associated with sampling and appropriation (Clover 2011, especially 89–90; see also Clover 2009, 25–50), and the video's musical backing track is accompanied by stock graphics that are cycled through by applying various changing color palettes in a veritable *tour de force* of the era's multimedia production standards. Indeed, one wonders to what extent the video and its soundtrack are composed out of fully licensed (or license-free) sources, or rather if its makers might instead perhaps claim fair use for at least some of the sampled drums and/or visual motifs it incorporates. Regardless, the video's existence is ultimately inseparable from the techniques of reproduction it decries, as digital logics of reproducibility are the cultural legacy to which producers and consumers alike are heir in the age of multimedia, which is perhaps why the focus here is less on the legal ramifications of piracy than its supposed economic and, ultimately, moral consequences.

To say that the commodity peaks with the advent of the shrink-wrapped software package is also to say that from there it goes into decline. Software, and software "publishing" specifically, does begin to disappear as the SPA predicted, but not as it feared. Screens do, in fact, begin to shrink and even fade as mobile devices and the embedded components that will make up the *Internet of Things* come to be the dominant computing platforms of the early 21st century, and programs themselves do seem to fall through a black hole as the commoditized software package is increasingly replaced with the *Software as a Service* (SaaS) paradigm. SaaS is generally conceived as a back-end phenomenon, powering platforms like Amazon Web Services and Microsoft Azure, on which other companies' software applications can run without the need for them to maintain a physical server infrastructure. Even more so, the term is used to describe a paradigm for constructing made-to-order applications, business processes, or workflows out of individual, constituent parts as, for example, with the widely popular Salesforce.

com, whose phone number is in fact listed on their website as 1-800-NO-SOFTWARE. Yet, today, with the retail software store practically nonexistent and the floppy itself a media-archeological relic, it is worth considering the ways in which the service paradigm has subsumed even shrink-wrapped end-user software.

In January 2015, for example, following its success in rebranding Office, arguably its most valuable software product, as a sub-scription service with Office 365, Microsoft announced that its forthcoming operating system, Windows 10, would be available under similar terms:

> We think of Windows as a Service – in fact, one could reasonably think of Windows in the next couple of years as one of the largest Internet services on the planet. (Meyerson 2015)

One could view this move in terms of the software giant playing catch-up to Apple, which has offered upgrades to its iOS mobile operating system free to those with a valid mobile carrier con-tract since the release of the original iPhone in 2007 and free upgrades to its desktop OS X operating system since 2013. Unlike the latter company, however, which could be said to take a more Kittlerian approach, subsidizing its OS development costs through the sale of hardware, Microsoft, which licenses Windows to third-party hardware manufacturers and thus relies directly on software sales for revenue, explicitly evokes the service paradigm as a justification for this transition. Where once new operating systems, most notably Windows 95, were met with customers queuing up to be the first to walk out the door with a boxed copy, the Windows as a Service paradigm suggests that even the software most fundamental to the operation of our personal computers is now considered something akin to infrastructure, maintained under contract rather than delivered as standalone product.

Free and *Open Source* software (F/OSS) has often been championed as a response to the shrink-wrapped commodity model, but the interventions that made it a powerful alternative to proprietary software have thus far proven largely ineffective in addressing the specific inequalities perpetuated by the expansion of capital via SaaS. Many of the requirements of the venerable GPL (*GNU General Public License*), such as the requirement to publicly offer source code (including any modifications made), do not apply to those running such software on a server that only presents the output of its computations to the end-user via the network, leaving these stipulations to the compatible, but less popular AGPL (*GNU Affero General Public License*, see GNU Operating System 2015). Exceptions like this allow "cloud" companies, including major tech players like Google and Apple, to take advantage of free software while maintaining the proprietary nature of their online services. Indeed, legal measures like the AGPL can only partially ameliorate this situation. GNU founder Richard Stallman describes the conundrum in terms of *Service as a Software Substitute* (SaaSS):

> [I]f the programs on the server are free that doesn't protect *the server's users* from the effects of SaaSS…SaaSS always subjects you to the power of the server operator, and the only remedy is, *Don't use SaaSS!* (Stallman 2010, emphases in original)

The service paradigm can thus be seen as supplanting not only commodity, but free software ideology as well.

Perhaps even more strikingly, Adobe Systems' 2013 move to a "Creative Cloud" infrastructure for its suite of multimedia software including Photoshop, Flash, and Illustrator replaces the shrink wrap model with a subscription service for the very group of "creative professionals" whose jobs, at least until the financial crisis of 2008, were seemingly one of the few bright spots in an otherwise bleak global economy. If, as Lori Emerson has argued, Apple has made of "creativity" something of a fetish, obscuring the very *lack* of creativity it fosters upon users through its increasingly closed software and hardware interfaces (Emerson 2014, 18-19), the Creative Cloud paradigm and its corresponding mobile apps suggest that even that limited amount of imagination is now only available on loan from major multinational corporations. Viewed in comparison with the origins of Photoshop, one of the Creative Cloud's (and, indeed, Adobe's) flagship products, the "Creativity as a Service" paradigm tracks the ongoing reduction of the so-called "creative class" (Florida 2002) to bonded laborers. Developed in the late 1980s and debuting as a 1.0 product in 1990, where it quickly became a cornerstone of the digital multimedia revolution, Photoshop is arguably the software product most responsible for the ascendance of this class in the first place: on a website recently constructed to celebrate the program's 25th anniversary, Hungarian artist and photographer Flora Borsi writes,

> When I was a young girl, I didn't have the money to organize shoots in a studio, so I created whatever I wanted in Photoshop. Thank you, Adobe, for giving me the tools and opportunity to build my career. (Adobe 2015)

Yet, in a Reddit *Ask Me Anything* with Photoshop co-creator Thomas Knoll scheduled as part of this celebration, one particular thread (amongst a handful of other mentions of the topic) remarked upon how crucial the role of piracy had been in developing children, who usually could not afford the famously expensive software, into paying adult professional users. User mkautzm writes,

> It's very indirect and it's definitely playing the long game, but if you can get teenagers invested in your product before it's actually time to make a purchasing decision either for a business or for personal use, I think that's extremely sustainable and profitable for a business...This is hugely at odds with the Adobe Cloud. (Reddit 2015)

As a method of shifting away from a commodity model that also carries with it the added benefit of being more closely able to contain piracy, SaaS, especially when extended into end-user software like Windows and Photoshop, offers an example of Thomas Piketty's much-celebrated analysis describing how a rentier economy flourishes when r, the rate of capital return, exceeds g, the rate of economic growth (Piketty 2014, 25–27 and 422–424), shifted into the "immaterial," digital realm. Correlative with a decline in career development and upward mobility, commercial software providers, rather than relying upon those who pirate a shrink-wrapped copy to develop into legitimate owners of subsequent major versions when they become financially and professionally solvent, now prefer to lease them as "services" to all users on a monthly or yearly basis in exchange for precarious, ever-revocable access to a steady stream of incremental updates.

Services in fact occupy something of a contradictory place in Piketty's analysis in that they simultaneously account, at least in Western economies, for the largest sector of economic growth over the past 200 years—one primarily based upon raw human labor such that "an hour's work of the typical wage-earner in the twenty-first century can buy just as many haircuts as an hour's work a hundred years ago" (Piketty 2014, 90)—yet, at the same time, one that contains "the lowest paid workers" (Piketty 2014, 280). In fact, he argues that services have become so dominant and such a catchall term that

> [i]t would probably be more perspicuous to group activities in terms of their ultimate purpose (health, transport, housing, etc.) and give up on the distinction agriculture/ industry/services. (Piketty 2014, 589, n. 17)

In much the same way that nearly all media are now digital, nearly everything is now a service, so the need to specifically identify them as such is superfluous; this is an expansion of auto-nomist Marxists Michael Hardt and Antonio Negri's assertion that what they call "immaterial labor has become *hegemonic in qualitative terms*" (Hardt and Negri 2004, 109, emphasis in original). The service sector, for them, is a subset of immaterial labor, which also includes logical and semantic practices such as programming, but in a SaaS economy, these distinctions are rapidly vanishing. With mobile applications like Uber, Airbnb, and TaskRabbit connecting contractually-independent drivers, part-time landlords (or sublessors), and contingent workers with paying customers, software becomes the means for the sup-posed "disintermediation" of buyers from sellers in an immaterial labor market more accurately defined in terms of service than "sharing."[4] With companies like Elance-oDesk and OnForce, this regime is extended to developers as the "Everything as a Service" model incorporates even the creation of software services themselves (DCR TrendLine 2014).

If the autonomist hope was that the qualitative hegemony of immaterial labor offered a turn away from the mystification of the commodity form and towards Marx's "social life-process" not through the disenchantments of the avant-garde but via the expanding multitude that capital attempts to subject to this potentially more self-evident regime of labor, then the (return of the) service economy in software, as the qualitative and quantitative expansion of an already-existing contingent labor force, represents capital's full-throated response to these con-ditions.[5] Services do make more apparent the social networks

4   On apps like Uber and Airbnb the provider is rated as much if not more than the amenities "shared." An Uber driver is not so much "sharing" her or his car as they are chauffeuring someone somewhere; in order to ensure a favorable rating on the site, an Airbnb "host" often, if not always, provides a variety of services (cleaning, cooking, potentially even companionship) above and beyond the strict "sharing" of lodging with his or her "guests."

5   It is important to note that the mainframe era of computing offered its own version of SaaS with companies like IBM complementing the sale or rental of their massive and costly hardware with development consulting services. The current SaaS model is thus in a sense both a return to and an expansion of this concept whereby it is extended from the enterprise to the population at large. For more on the multitude, see Hardt and Negri (2004).

that constitute labor relations, but they do so while taking an invisible, yet hefty cut. Indeed, this is Piketty's point when he highlights the absurdity inherent in the president of the European Central Bank's campaign against "rents":

> What the central banker had in mind, apparently, was lack of competition in the service sector: taxi drivers, hairdressers, and the like were presumably making too much money. The problem posed by this use of the word 'rent' is very simple: the fact that capital yields income, which in accordance with the original meaning of the word we refer to...as 'annual rent produced by capital,' has absolutely nothing to do with the problem of imperfect competition or monopoly. (Piketty 2014, 423)

Capital, in other words, extracts rent regardless of the licensed professions it seeks to disrupt in the name of "efficiency," and software-enabled service economy companies like the taxi-supplanting Uber are nothing more than the way it does so at their expense. Thus, if it seems that, in a sense, there is no (longer any) software, it is not through its reduction to the pure potential of the universal machine, but by way of its hypostatization into the agent of universal economic exchange, the ultimate mediator of social relations and the ultimate aim of globalization. Similarly, when everything becomes a service, humanity can no longer be considered to be approaching a common existence as unalienated beings marshaling the free *potentia* of our collective labor; rather, everyone becomes a serf. Just as information security analyst Graham Cluley has suggested, echoing Stallman, that we ought to replace the word "cloud" with the phrase "somebody else's computer" (Palmer 2013), when we hear the word "service" we should instead think "somebody else's property," a deniable reality as long as we still had a chance of convincing ourselves that it was we who had ownership over the contents of a box, rather than the other way 'round.

Bibliography

Adobe. 2015. "25 Years of Photoshop." *Adobe Systems, Inc*. Accessed February, 22 2015. http://www.adobe.com/products/photoshop/25-year-anniversary.html.

Benjamin, Walter. 1968. "The Work of Art in the Age of Mechanical Reproduction" (1936). In Walter Benjamin, *Illuminations*, edited by Hannah Arendt. Translated by Harry Zohn, 217–251. New York, NY: Schocken.

Clover, Joshua. 2009. *1989: Bob Dylan Didn't Have This to Sing About*. Berkeley, CA: University of California Press.

Clover, Joshua. 2011. "Ambiguity and Theft." In *Cutting Across Media: Appropriation Art, Interventionist College, and Copyright Law,* edited by Kembrew McLeod and Rudolf Kuenzli, 84–93. Durham, NC: Duke University Press.

DCR TrendLine. 2014. "Everything-as-a-Service." Accessed April, 6 2015. http://trendline.dcrworkforce.com/everythingasaservice.html.

Emerson, Lori. 2014. *Reading Writing Interfaces: From the Digital to the Bookbound*. Minneapolis, MN: University of Minnesota Press.

Florida, Richard. 2002. *The Rise of the Creative Class: And How It's Transforming Work, Leisure, Community and Everyday Life*. New York, NY: Basic Books.

Galloway, Alexander R., and Eugene Thacker. 2007. *The Exploit: A Theory of Networks*. Minneapolis, MN: University of Minnesota Press.

GNU Operating System. "Why the Affero GPL." Accessed April, 5 2015. https://www.gnu.org/licenses/why-affero-gpl.html.

Hardt, Michael and Antonio Negri. 2004. *Multitude: War and Democracy in the Age of Empire*. London: Penguin.

Horspool, R. Nigel, and N. Marovac. 1980. "An Approach to the Problem of Detranslation of Computer Programs." *The Computer Journal* 23 (3): 223–229.

Jameson, Fredric. 1991. *Postmodernism, or, The Cultural Logic of Late Capitalism*. Durham, NC: Duke University Press.

Kittler, Friedrich. 1995. "There is no Software." *CTHEORY*. Accessed 21 February 2015. http://www.ctheory.net/articles.aspx?id=74.

Mandel, Ernest. 1978. *Late Capitalism* (1972). Translated by Joris De Bres. London: Verso.

Manovich, Lev. 2001. *The Language of New Media*, Cambridge, MA: MIT Press.

Marx, Karl. 1976. *Capital: A Critique of Political Economy, Volume One* (1867). Translated by Ben Fowkes. London: Penguin.

Meyerson, Terry. 2015. "The next generation of Windows: Windows 10." *Blogging Windows*. Accessed February, 22 2015. http://blogs.windows.com/bloggingwindows/2015/01/21/the-next-generation-of-windows-windows-10/.

Palmer, Danny. 2013. "We should replace the word 'cloud' with 'somebody else's computer', says security expert." *Computing*. Accessed February, 25 2015. http://www.computing.co.uk/ctg/news/2316368/we-should-replace-the-word-cloud-with-somebody-elses-computer-says-security-expert.

Piketty, Thomas. 2014. *Capital in the 21st Century* (2013). Translated by Arthur Goldhammer. Cambridge, MA: The Belknap Press of Harvard University Press.

Reddit. 2015. "Hi everyone, I'm Thomas Knoll and 25 years ago this week I co-founded Photoshop with my brother John. AMA." Accessed February, 22 2015. http://www.reddit.com/r/IAmA/comments/2wh6fx/hi_everyone_im_thomas_knoll_and_25_years_ago_this.

Shannon, Claude. 1949. "Communication Theory of Secrecy Systems." *The Bell System Technical Journal* 28 (4): 656–715.

The Software Publishers Association. 1992. "Don't Copy That Floppy." Directed by M. J. Vilardi. Lyrics by M. E. Hart.

Stallman, Richard. 2010. "Who does that server really serve?" *Boston Review*, March 18. Accessed May 28, 2015. Repr. *GNU Operating System*. Accessed April, 5 2015. https://www.gnu.org/philosophy/who-does-that-server-really-serve.html.

Sterne, Jonathan. 2012. *MP3: The Meaning of a Format.* Durham, NC: Duke University Press.

Tsing, Anna Lowenhaupt. 2005. *Friction: An Ethnography of Global Connection.* Princeton, NJ: Princeton University Press.

DATABASE

LABOR

BLACK BOX POLITICS

LOGISTICS

ORGANIZATIONAL CULTURES

Service Orientations: Data, Institutions, Labor

Liam Magee and Ned Rossiter

Our central interest in this essay is to consider the role of the database as a technology of governance and the scramble of power as it relates to a capacity to model the world and exert influence upon it. We argue Software as a Service is more than a new vogue term of the IT industry, constituting a longer temporal horizon and more complex rearrangement of relations between data and labor to which the database and its entailments remain critical.

Arguably the *relational database* has had greater impact on the transformation of organizational cultures and the world economy than the Internet. The analytic potential of computational databases coupled with the materiality of data centers has produced models of this world without historical precedent. Key here is the question of scale and the ubiquity of data capture. The structuring of data has a genealogy. The knowledge once derived from the transitional technologies of cabinets of curiosities (*Wunderkammer*), demographic registries and Foucault's "great tables" in the 17th and 18th centuries—later systematized into various epistemic instruments that included Diderot's encyclopaedia, the periodic table, the museum and Linnaeus' taxonomies—were all coincident with the rise of populations governed as statistical subjects. The Cartesian grid, a two-dimensional space for organization and arrangement, provided an abstract template for subsequent techniques to employ in the structuring and querying of data. Such instruments can today be understood as proto-databases, foreshadowing what Gernot Böhme has called our present era of "invasive technification" (Böhme 2012).

Critique and judgement become hoodwinked by the seemingly irrefutable authority of statistics and visualizations of the incomprehensible. Decisions are made on the basis of a misrecognition between data and the material world. Cognition is now outsourced to the machine. Leibniz's dream of a *mathesis universalis* becomes in this incarnation a nightmarish inversion—from being at the center of the modern epistemological enterprise, humans are now peripheral data collectors and, increasingly, just data. Structurally oblivious to their function in the reproduction of value within an economy of data, the human has entered a new period of machinic arrangement whose operation is abstracted into the realm of semiotic capitalism (Lazzarato 2014). An imaginary of cooperation, sharing and participation provides a powerful narrative for the entrepreneurial-self whose capacity to organize collective forms of refusal is consistently undermined by

the disaggregating effects of value extraction derived from the
computational logic of recombination hidden within the vaults of
algorithmic architectures (Scholz 2014; Terranova 2014).

The advent of the relational database in the early seventies marks
a critical transition in the ductility and malleability of knowledge
of people and populations. Edgar Codd, an IBM employee, first
introduced the relational model as an alternative to existing network and hierarchical database systems. The relational database
differs by formalizing the relationships between the logical
elements contained in distinct sets; one of its advantageous
effects was to separate the operations of manipulating and
querying data from its physical location on hard drives (Codd
1970). The cost and time involved in changing how programs work
with data is accordingly reduced. The interrogation of subjects
soon after becomes literalised with the advent of the *Structured
English Query Language*, or SEQUEL (and later SQL), in a paper
by Chamberlin and Boyce, also IBM employees, in 1974. Already
the human subject is captured in specific "relations" of labor and
commodities. Chamberlain and Boyce's very first example con-
sists of a "relation describing employees," featuring the barely
fictional cast of familiar surnames: "Jones," "Smith" and "Lee"
(1974, 250). A further example of query references equally familiar
brands: "Find those items which are supplied by Levi and sold
in the men's department" (253). These examples also betray the
spatial and cultural centers of the fledgling IT industry.

With the advent of the relational model and SQL, information
becomes in a new sense purely programmable as data and
available for, among other things, forms of *ad hoc* knowledge
production. It opens up entirely new scientific fields of informatics. Data mining, business intelligence, real-time analytics,
customer relationship management (CRM) and enterprise
resource planning (ERP) are unthinkable without the modern
database. This in turn has led to a technological shift in the
processing and logistical operations of modern institutions,
with transformative effects in the apparently mundane fields of

report writing, insurance assessment, credit checks and policy development. What were once specialized arts become template-driven and eminently replicable institutional processes.

Here, knowledge rubs up against the politics of parameters. New uses of data became a constant in the social life of institutional settings, laden with a politics that remains for the most part implicit as it is pervasive. As Codd noted presciently, though without apparent concern for its political implications, "future users of large data banks must be protected from having to know how the data is organized in the machine" (Codd 1970, 377). Implied here is a system operating in "protected mode," a form of prophylactic for organizers of the data as well as for those "future users" at risk of going crazy (Kittler 2013). As Friedrich Kittler observes, the power of the *protected mode* is "derived ... from the efficacy of silence" (Kittler 2013, 213). Unable to intervene in the *operating system* (OS) of the machine, the user is locked out from issuing commands that alter the architecture and addressable memory special to the *real mode* of Intel's x86 *central processing unit* (CPU) introduced in 1978. Intel's 80286 16-bit microprocessor, released in 1982, distinguished between real mode and protected mode, a CPU designed for multitasking applications operating in real-time secured by increased operating system control.[1] Modern operating systems, Windows, MacOS and Linux, continue to use this mode to protect us from our machines, in some sense, even today.

The widespread adoption of protected mode systems impacts upon the economy of expression, practice, subjectivity and knowledge. In one of his rare moments of invoking a concept of power, Kittler suggests that the Foucauldian analysis be reoriented around an investigation of how protected modes

---

1   Kittler's object of critique is the 80386 32-bit microprocessor released in 1985, which improved upon the protected mode of the 80286 by allowing mode-switching. The 80386 also had greater market penetration and was widely adopted across a range of institutional settings.

specific to technological systems and their "privileges" provide
the key to reconstructing the transformation of bureaucracies.
While not renowned for political statements, Kittler considers the
issue of access rights as, in effect, the new front of a geopolitical
war against the hegemony of the United States and the imperial
extension of its IT industry across global economy and society.

One might reasonably assert that *Open Source* software (OSS)
offers such an alternative to protected mode. But for the most
part, OSS mimics if not aspires to the aesthetic regime of the
hugely dominant operating systems. Do-it-yourself (DIY) hardware assembly might offer a more deviant alternative, though
even moreso than OSS it is unable to scale up to pose any real
challenge to the IT behemoths. The DIY hardware movement
is increasingly tied to maker culture, which as the long-tail
of "artisan-alternatives" is not prepared to admit how the
valorization of localism frequently depends on global supply
chains (Wark 2013). Virtuous acts of rarefied consumption
coupled with the satisfaction of self-assembly fulfill a hipster
imaginary of distinction, an inner-city latte variation on IKEA.
Just as the imaginary itself is part of a global media production,
reverberating from one trendy alleyway to another, its desires are
serviced through the concealed operations of the world logistical
economy.

The OSS and maker cultures encompass a spectrum from "com-
plicit" corporate-backed organizations (for example, the Apache
Software Foundation) through to iconoclasts and hacktivists who
offer some scope for critical kick-back. While the OSS movement
in general shares an obvious alignment with the call by Kittler
(and many others) for forms of open access, or real mode, this
does not disqualify the scepticism we register here. Even the
most idealistic of projects can become entangled in corporatism.
MySQL is a widely used database system, a "poster child" of the
OSS movement and the default for many other OSS projects,
including the popular blogging engine WordPress. In 2008 the
Swedish firm that hosted and supported MySQL was sold to Sun

Microsystems, which in turn was soon after acquired by Oracle, the largest vendor of enterprise database systems in the world. It continues to be supported by Oracle as a means of "upselling" users to its more expensive suite of products. In protest, one of the founders of MySQL then launched a Save MySQL campaign (Wikipedia contributors 2015).

The durability of knowledge practices was and continues to be coextensive with the persistence of parameters. Political existence contracts into the embodiment of Quine's dictum: to be is to be the value of a variable. Manuel DeLanda has, in another context, reflected explicitly upon the conceptual individuation of the assemblage through a process of parametrizing, or "providing it with 'knobs' with modifiable settings the values of which determine the condition of the identity of an emergent whole at any given time" (DeLanda 2011, 187). Just as contemporary philosophy is tempted, then, to think entire ontologies, including social systems, through the affordances of database logics, the operations of modern institutional life and labor are equally determined by processes of parametric adjustment, tuning and tweaking. Changing these values—the settings of parameters—alters the configuration of thought and practice.

By the early 1980s the increasing reliance of all institutions on the parametric affordances of the database reinforces and reinflects late twentieth century theories of institutionalism. For Max Weber, operating under earlier assumptions about the institution, it appeared as a necessarily constrained artefact of capitalist modernity, a comparatively inflexible and non-configurable organizational form without parameters (Weber 1930). In announcing "new institutionalism," Paul DiMaggio and Walter Powell revisited this "iron cage of bureaucracy," reconceiving the modern institutional form as instead an "isomorphic" entity with shared common procedures, structures and operational norms which at the same time could be capable of adaptation to geographic, commercial and industry-specific conditions (DiMaggio and Powell 1983). We argue this isomorphism or "elective affinity"

between organizational forms and techno-materialist conditions
at particular conjunctures is recognizable by new institutionalist
theorists in part due to its historical coincidence with the ubiquity
and relatively enduring quality of the enterprise database. In the
same way, the onset of flexible modes of capital accumulation
was not a transformation independent of emergent developments in computational architectures. The logistical world
of what Anna Tsing (2009) terms "supply chain capitalism" has
become increasingly governed largely by the dual and interconnected processes of real-time computationality and just-in-time
modes of production and distribution. The agility of the modern
institution is, then, contingent upon the combinatory possibilities
of relational databases that operate at ever increasing scales.

Since the 2000s the capacity for institutions to adapt to regimes
of flexibilization is augmented, rather than replaced, by novel
non-relational systems. So-called NoSQL, or *non-relational
databases*, appear to relax the constraints imposed by the
relational model. Seemingly new paradigms of data management add further layers of what Codd had termed "protective"
indirection between users and the physical allocation of zeroes
and ones on magnetic or solid state hard drives. Two particular
IT terms resonate here: SaaS, or *Software as a Service*, and SOA,
or *Service-oriented Architecture*. The first term, SaaS, refers to the
delivery of software as a series of features, or *services*, over a
network rather than as an executable file that installs and runs
from a computer's hard disk. The second, SOA, describes instead
a way of developing software to expose critical functions, again
as services, over a network for use by other software. Databases
do not disappear in these frameworks. Rather, they are transformed into services provided to other systems, other services
and part of a larger combinatory puzzle through which clients,
both machinic and human, have their informatic demands met.
In theory, organizations providing such computational services
are interchangeable. In practice, IT language such as standards
compliance, consumer choice and the ability to plug-and-play

different services and vendors become tokens in a game of entrenchment that pays lip service to flexibility. Choice is seen through the prism of constrained parameters. This logic refracts the insular world of IT fashions and policies to the larger fields of institutional labor and politics, increasingly dependent upon these apparent abstractions of informational architectures.

Part of the flexibility of what Stefano Harney and Fred Moten term the "algorithmic institution" tasked with the management of "logistical populations" is immanent to the technical operation of enterprise databases such as Oracle and IBM, which are prone to bugs, hardware malfunctions, software glitches and the like (Harney and Moten 2013, 90–91; Harney 2014). Yet the logistical fantasy of a smooth world of seamless interoperability is not disturbed by technical malfunctions alone. As Harney and Moten write:

> Every attempt by logistics to dispel strategy, to banish human time, to connect without going through the subject, to subject without handling things, resists something that is already resisting it, namely the resistance that founds modern logistics. (Harney and Moten 2013, 91–92)

Logistics is always troubled by that which it cannot obtain, by the indeterminate temporal and spatial horizons and hidden reserves of human subjectivity that forever entice the technocratic tendency with the promise enhanced measures of efficiency, yet which by definition remain beyond the calibrating optic of logistics. This is why so much cognitive attention and so many financial resources are expended upon designing more complex computational infrastructures.

"The Service Orientation"

In the first decades of the relational database, it was possible to imagine this tool of bureaucratic enlargement through the metaphor of the physical container. Sitting in air-conditioned windowless rooms, database servers retained a tenuous but palpable link between the logical and the physical. Databases ran on big iron mainframes or industrial-strength PCs capable of fast input/output operations, low disk and network latency, and high transactional throughput and parallelism. Data had a home; it could be secured, locked down, contained within the appropriately named data center. Deeply nested behind non-descript suburban office exteriors and warehouses, technicians and administrators, with talents that were obscure even to the broader IT industry, kept the machines and data systems humming. Yet the prospect of fully automated labor was never far from the machine dreams surrounding the database. Robots took over the swapping of back-up tapes; self-replicating and load-balancing databases reduced the need for human monitoring.

This is not so much a story of manufacturing and low-wage jobs offshored to developing economies; such features can also be found in the majority of advanced economies. Rather, the integration of multiple layers of value-generating activities is made coincident as a result of technologies of governance such as the relational database. Labor becomes increasingly sub-ject to the logistical regime of real-time coordination, command and control. In an inversion of the processes of software and database design techniques used to simulate "real world" objects such as the "customer" or the "employee," *pace* Chamberlin and Boyce (1974), these labor entities begin to resemble more and more the data structures of enterprise resource planning and human resource (HR) systems they are supposedly modeled upon (Rossiter 2015).

Beginning in the nineties, but maturing with the arrival in the mid-2000s of fully-fledged virtualized or *cloud* services such as Amazon Web Services and EC2 (Elastic Compute Cloud), Microsoft's Azure platform and Google's App Engine, SOAs pose a radically alternative computing paradigm. At the same time this paradigm looks to extends Codd's desire to "protect" users still further. Housed on highly virtualized farms of servers in data centers, databases could now reside everywhere—and nowhere. What matters under this paradigm is no longer the specific configuration of technical data structures to physical hard drives and machines, but rather the relations, tuples, lists, sets, sequences, keys and tables peculiar to the processing of data. Indeed, the modern database administrator, including the humble maintainer of WordPress websites, is less and less likely to understand how these relations are configured at all. Rather, the database exists, increasingly, as a kind of implied contract to supply its clients with a range of data services, delivered over networks using various standardized protocols that include SOAP (*Simple Object Access Protocol*) or REST (*Representational State Transfer*).

The database is no longer a container, a tangible housing or repository. Instead, it is service oriented: the passive object of a sentence, that which is responsive to requests. From the point of view of the demanding client, it is no longer relevant whether these service requests are resolved by a tightly coordinated cluster of processes running on the same processor, or instead, and increasingly, by a loosely federated web of interconnected services. In effect, this means the architecture is never questioned. Any plea for change or deeper level access is met with resounding indifference by the proprietors of control. The function of the client is to submit to service. Such a technique of capture provides the basis for scalar expansion. One may choose to migrate to other providers, but the time and cost associated with adapting organizational processes and activities to slightly reconfigured architectures is significant. So no matter how much a client may wish to flee service-oriented systems, the operational indebtedness to a particular architecture more often exceeds the will to escape. In spite of the rhetoric of standards compliance and migration pathways, in practice user "protection" risks becoming pacification.

The devolution of computing to the shapelessness of the cloud is one of the IT industry's recurring motifs. Even if it is not inevitable, there is nonetheless a danger in exaggerating the convergence between networks, storage and computational processes. Already by 1984 it was plausible to market the idea that "the network is the computer" (Olsen 2008; Aytes 2012). Similarly, in 2015, it is also possible to argue that the compelling story of reified services, both in the purely computational sense of SOA and in the economic derivation of SaaS and its near-cognates, *Infrastructure as a Service* (IaaS) and *Platform as a Service* (PaaS), has long since subsided into the background noise of general IT hardware and software commoditization. These technologies have reached their point of design stasis, what in Gartner's jargon would be termed the "plateau of productivity."

Yet the terminology of computing services suggests a more meaningful turn, a re-orientation is underway. Through the prism of the new computing service industries—which include not only the outsourcing of hardware, software and network capacity, but also quasi-human services such as system monitoring and back-up, fault detection and data analytics—it is possible to imagine a highly compressed history of capitalism replayed at a rapidly accelerated velocity. It is as though computing, having earlier exorcised its primary and secondary industry moments, is today running headlong into its post-industrial epoch—an event heralded for capitalism at large only in the 1970s. Aping the age of corporatism, of endless outsourcing, offshoring, vertical and horizontal integration, mergers, acquisitions and divestments of non-core assets, the rise of the global SOA effaces as meaningless the authority of the singular, coherent software system or repository of data. The tangible data product—a hard drive, a floppy disk, a memory stick—is now fully transformed into an etherealized thing, an intangible commodity, an abstract service, often performed either algorithmically or supported via data entry by nimble fingers or server maintenance from bodies in spaces remote to the sites of consumption.

The newly formed fabric of SaaS represents, then, the realization of a particular logic of procedural alienation—a realization in which both the computational time of processing cycles and human programmatic labor of developing services lose their distinctiveness. In this model, "Software as a Product" disappears. So too does the appealing cottage industry of eighties shareware culture, swap meets, and the then-fledgling Open Source movement, where at least the programmer's authorship and reputation could be tied—however superficially, and now, with some sense of nostalgia—to an identifiable artefact or commodity. In its place comes a grey world of interconnected service endpoints, undifferentiated, integrated and distinguished only by IP addresses and a coded declaration of their capabilities.

This architectural model has its political analogue in the rise of microwork, exemplified by another Amazon site: the Mechanical Turk (MT). [2] Here, for the remaining low-value services algorithms cannot quite yet accommodate, and which need therefore to be especially qualified as Human Intelligence Tasks (or HITs), it is possible to buy and sell human labor at piece-meal rates. The original eighteenth century Turk represented a machine that dissembled the rules specific to its operation, all the while being driven by human labor. The Amazon "refresh" suggests a new possibility: human labor now fills in the gaps for those cases where algorithms are insufficient. Tasks include identifying duplicate Facebook and Google+ accounts, labelling materials of objects in photographs and deciphering handwriting (Limer 2014). This form of service orientation is, today, a fortunately esoteric form of soliciting labor. Yet the close approximation in language and function between Amazon's EC2 and Mechanical Turk—both promote the flexibility of "elastic" resources—offers a glimpse of a degree of "invasive technification" that exceeds the gloomy predictions of Böhme. The algorithmic possibilities of the service-oriented institution are similarly elastic: they continue to stretch and expand across a range of human occupations, a process of

labor automation decried since the seventeenth century (see
Hobsbawm 1952).

Moving into the twenty-first century, it is not so much the
threat of obsolescence as the disappearance of boundaries and
responsibilities that, paradoxically, is presaged by the rise of the
SOA-led institutions. It becomes increasingly difficult to see in
the current orientation towards services how from the point of
view of the service consumer certain forms of monotonous and
metric-laden human labor can be differentiated any longer from
those performed by computers. The work of Business Process
Outsourcing (BPO) has become a staple economy across much
of the IT sector in India. Servicing the needs of data entry in the
medical, insurance, logistical and finance sectors for both large
multi-national companies and Small and Medium Enterprises
(SMEs), BPO work is secure as long as wages remain suppressed.
Like the circuit board that never tires, BPO work and its affective
correlate found in call centers is 24/7 both offer a form of
"sensory impoverishment" that dulls perception and dissipates
any reserves of energy that might be harnessed into forms of
labor organizing (Crary 2013, 33, 105).

The Ethereal Database, or, Black Box Politics

If the relational database represents the institutional transition
to a computational form of modernism, where paper records
were replaced by tuples identified by a primary key and assem-
bled into new kinds of "great tables," then now we are arguably
entering into an era of the hypermodern. When information loses
its anchorage in physical analogues of filing and record keeping
systems and succumbs to a new set of dissolvent metaphorical
clusters—of *cloud computing*, agile methods, mobile devices,
virtual machines and an elasticity of resource provisioning
(computational or human)—it loses its last vestiges of tangibility.
Adopting Lewis Mumford's metaphor of technology, it can be said
to have become "etherealized" (Mumford 1938). For Mumford,

the city was a space where, in a strange shifting of metaphors, information "'etherealized' through the city into *durable* elements in the human heritage" (Mumford 1938, 3, emphasis added). In a quite different sense, the information space once occupied by the relational database can similarly be thought of as something in a hybrid state: simultaneously dissolving, becoming elusive, transparent, ethereal and also gathering in insulated and protective layers, unknowable, a machinic servant receiving inputs and responding with outputs. The black box is at once opaque and utterly transparent.

While "vaporware" indicates software that is so soft that it in fact does nothing, or does not exist, we can imagine an alternative coinage in which the metaphors of ether and vapor infuse with that of a new term like cloud computing. But it is not only the ethereal quality of data management that concerns us here. Such attributes are, as we have suggested, part of the hype machine special to the IT industry and its services. Database records still need to be inscribed as zeroes and ones on magnetic or solid state discs, which are usually located in largely inaccessible data centers. What becomes difficult to think here is the simultaneous properties of ethereal transparency and material opacity that attend the new data services. The commercial enclosure of communications infrastructure coupled with the opacity of algorithmic architectures special to SaaS gives rise to a politics of the black box.

For the data-dependent enterprise this signals, in the first instance, a calculable trade-off between direct control and efficiencies and economies of scale. By shearing off its dependency on "big iron" mainframe computing to service providers while continuing to transact in "big data," the modern institution simultaneously divests yet another no-longer-core activity—managing its own data—while insinuating itself yet further into the unstable set of relations that cut across old institutional lines. Here, the term "architecture," always metaphorically overladen when applied to software, is instead completely misleading, vanishing into its opposite: a destructured network of loosely coordinated endpoints, refracting service requests and responses from point to point. The possibility for error is accordingly amplified; the responsibility for that error lost, along with any single locus of control over computational results. If, as Jaron Lanier recently suggested, "the distinction between a corporation and an algorithm is fading," under the distributed scenarios of a fully realized SOA/SaaS digital economy even the "algorithm" is no longer singular nor self-contained (Brockman 2014). With the rise of smart cities one finds an increasing feedback operation in which "all that is solid" modulates forms of algorithmic governance and vice-versa. Adaptation and transformation is a mutually constitutive process contained, retrieved and acted upon within the parameters of the database that is now oriented towards an architecture of service delivery. The *SOA database* would be a crude approximation to this concept of data that is no longer "based" anywhere.

In the broad advent of the SOA/SaaS digital economy any organization can avail itself of "elastic" data facilities at seemingly any scale. Any organization can make use of predictive analytics, business intelligence and a host of ancillary services for data authentication, search, logging, billing, monitoring, visualization, conversion, publication and backup. And while these services may be offered in limited variety, by a limited range of vendors, any organization can also differentiate itself through the large combinatory possibilities that an even seemingly small number of parameters provides. The relational database ushered in new forms of predictive and just-in-time data analytics through the ability to develop *ad hoc* queries and reports, thereby allowing modern institutions simultaneously to become homogenized as a general form while differentiated in parametric specificity. The SOA database accelerates both sets of tendencies towards institutional similitude and differentiation. Like the limitless possibilities a finite set of rules provides in the game of chess, the SOA database offers an infinitude of institutional forms to emerge within the horizon of its parameters. Similarly, it further accelerates the condition and precarity of service-oriented labor, setting new "standards" for how capital is flexibly accumulated and deployed. But where such institutional variation does occur, it is not reducible to the determining form of the database. Culture leaks beyond the structural constraints of data parameters. At the same time the processes of structural decoupling and disaggregation we describe above also introduce new prospects for self-cannibalization, creative destruction and systemic intervention. How to operate outside such limits and invent new systems of organization and cultures of expression will comprise a parametric politics of the present.

Bibliography

Aytes, Ayhan. 2012. "Return of the Crowds: Mechanical Turk and Neoliberal States of Exception." In *Digital Labor: The Internet as Playground and Factory*, edited by Trebor Scholz, 79–97. New York, NY: Routledge.

Böhme, Gernot. 2012. *Invasive Technification: Critical Essays in the Philosophy of Technology*. Translated by Cameron Shingleton. London; New York, NY: Bloomsbury.

Brockman, John. 2014. "The Myth of AI: A Conversation with Jaron Lanier." *Edge*, November 4. Accessed May 27, 2015. http://edge.org/conversation/the-myth-of-ai.

Chamberlin, Donald and Boyce, Raymond. 1974. "SEQUEL: A Structured English Query Language." *Proceedings of the 1974 ACM SIGFIDET (now SIGMOD) workshop on Data description, access and control*: 249–264.

Codd, Edgar F. 1970. "A Relational Model of Data for Large Shared Data Banks." *Communications of the ACM* 13 (6): 377–387.

Crary, Jonathan. 2013. *24/7: Late Capitalism and the Ends of Sleep*. London; New York: Verso.

DeLanda, Manuel. 2011. *Philosophy and Simulation: The Emergence of Synthetic Reason*. New York, NY: Continuum.

DiMaggio, Paul J., and Powell, Walter M. 1983. "The Iron Cage Revisited: Institutional Isomorphism and Collective Rationality in Organizational Fields." *American Sociological Review* 48 (2): 147–160.

Harney, Stefano. 2014. "Istituzioni algoritmiche e capitalismo logistico ('Algorithmic Institutions and Logistical Capitalism')." In *Gli algoritmi del capitale. Accelerazionismo, macchine della conoscenza e autonomia del comune (Algorithms of Capital: Accelerationism, Knowledge Machines and the Autonomy of the Common)*, edited by Matteo Pasquinelli, 116–129. Verona: Ombre Corte.

Harney, Stefano and Moten, Fred. 2013. *The Undercommons: Fugitive Planning & Black Study*. New York, NY: Minor Compositions.

Hobsbawm, Eric. 1952. "The Machine Breakers." *Past & Present* 1: 57–70. Accessed May 27, 2015. http://libcom.org/history/machine-breakers-eric-hobsbawm.

Kittler, Friedrich A. 2013. "Protected Mode." In *The Truth of the Technological World: Essays on the Genealogy of Presence*. Translated by Erik Butler, 209–218. Stanford, CA: Stanford University Press.

Lazzarato, Maurizio. 2014. *Signs and Machines: Capitalism and the Production of Subjectivity*. Translated by Joshua David Jordan. Los Angeles, CA: Semiotext(e).

Limer, Eric. 2014. "My Brief and Curious Life As a Mechanical Turk." *Gizmodo*, October 20. Accessed May 27, 2015. http://gizmodo.com/my-brief-and-curious-life-as-a-mechanical-turk-1587864671.

Mumford, Lewis. 1938. *The Culture of Cities*. San Diego, CA: Harcourt.

Olsen, Stefanie. 2008. "Sun's John Gage joins Al Gore in clean-tech investing." *CNET*, June 9. Accessed May 26, 2015. http://www.cnet.com/news/suns-john-gage-joins-al-gore-in-clean-tech-investing/.

Rossiter, Ned. 2015. "Coded Vanilla: Logistical Media and the Determination of Action." *South Atlantic Quarterly* 114 (1): 135–152.

Scholz, Trebor. 2014. "Platform Cooperativism vs. the Sharing Economy." *Medium*, December 5. Accessed May 27, 2015. https://medium.com/@trebors/platform-cooperativism-vs-the-sharing-economy-2ea737f1b5ad.

Terranova, Tiziana. 2014. "Red Stack Attack! Algorithms, Capital and the Automation of the Common." *Quaderni di San Precario*, February 14. Accessed May 27, 2015. http://quaderni.sanprecario.info/2014/02/red-stack-attack-algorithms-capital-and-the-automation-of-the-common-di-tiziana-terranova/.

The New School. 2014. "Digital Labour: Sweatshops, Picket Lines, Barricades." Conference at The Department of Media, New York City, NY, November 14–16. Accessed May 27, 2015. http://digitallabor.org/.

Tsing, Anna. 2009. "Supply Chains and the Human Condition." *Rethinking Marxism* 21 (2): 148–176.

Wark, McKenzie. 2013. "A More Lovingly Made World." *Cultural Studies Review* 19 (1): 296–304. Accessed May 27, 2015. http://epress.lib.uts.edu.au/journals/index.php/csrj/article/view/3170/3454.

Weber, Max. 1930. *The Protestant Ethic and the Spirit of Capitalism*. London: Allen & Unwin.

Wikipedia contributors. 2015. "MySQL: History." *Wikipedia: The Free Encyclopedia*. Last modified May 27, 2015, 12:00 CET. Accessed May 27, 2015. http://en.wikipedia.org/wiki/MySQL#History.

MOBILE APPS

APPLE

CLOUD COMPUTING

APP STORE

SOFTWARE AS A SERVICE

The Cloud, the Store, and Millions of Apps

Anders Fagerjord

The 1.5 million apps for the iPhone can be used
for thousands of purposes. Many are cloud-based
services, even more are games and simple utilities.
The idea of Software as a Service is to have one
instance of a program running on a central server,
and only one browser to access these programs.
From mobile devices it is more effective to access
services from apps than from browsers, meaning
that every user will need many apps. Moreover, hardware sensors are equally or more important to apps
than cloud access. Rather than thinking of apps as
software services, we should describe them as actors
in a network where developers, users, and Apple's
hardware, programming environment and App Store
are important parts.

"The Web is Dead" was the slogan that covered the entire front page of *Wired* in August, 2010. Mobile apps provide "simpler, sleeker services that just work," editor Chris Anderson wrote (2010b). Tim O'Reilly responded that "it's the backend that matters," pointing to the fact that popular services like Twitter, Google, or Facebook are run in large server centres which can be reached from web sites and native apps alike (Anderson 2010a). These servers, called the *cloud*, are used by many of the most popular apps. We store our documents and data in the cloud, sometimes sharing it in social networks, sometimes keeping it private. They are available to us from any screen we use, from the little telephone and the mid-sized tablet to the desktop computer and even the 50-inch TV screen. We still call them telephones and TVs, but we use them for the same services. It is the cloud, the backend, that matters, it seems.

Parts of the cloud, or some clouds to be more precise, are *Software as a Service* (SaaS) sites, where users can access computer systems running in central data centres. Instead of installing the software on their own machines, users access the systems through a web page. In my university, I file my travel expenses in one web site, read and write formal correspondence in another, and write drafts of papers with colleagues in Google Docs, which is also a web site. All are accessible from a *thin client*, my Web browser. As the thin client already is in my computer (and virtually all other computers) I only need to keep that one program up to date, and do not need to install and upgrade a lot of others. It is presumably easier for me, and it saves the university's computer department the work with purchasing upgrades and distributing them to all employees. The main system exists in only one instalment in the data centre, and may be updated at any time, without the need to distribute copies to all users.

Most of the time, however, I find that the web sites are slow and generally difficult to use. I often long for "simpler, sleeker services that just work," to borrow Anderson's words once more.

While desktop computers increasingly are used to access remote
software via a Web browser, mobile platforms are used without
the browser, instead favoring a myriad of native apps. We will
untangle this somewhat in the following, and realize early that
the *cloud* is a nice, simple metaphor for a complex actor network.
A short essay like this can hardly treat one network, let alone
several competing networks, so I will focus on apps made for
Apple's iOS, running on iPhones and iPads.

To describe a complex network like this, we need to be careful
in the use of words, especially as a term may be understood
differently by different sets of actors.

For a programmer, an *app* is an abbreviation for any application
program. Here, we will use app as in a more restricted sense,
which we believe is more in line with everyday language: an app is
a small program for a mobile device, downloaded from a central
distributor, an app store.

The term *service* is crucial for a book on SaaS. Here, we will have
to move away from the everyday understanding of service,
and limit it to the use within *Service-oriented Architecture* (SOA)
engineering, as defined by The Open Group:

> A service is a logical representation of a repeatable business
> activity that has a specified outcome (e.g., check customer
> credit, provide weather data, consolidate drilling reports,
> etc.) and: is self-contained, may be composed of other
> services, is a 'black box' to consumers of the service. (The
> Open Group 2013)

It should be added that these services are made available over
a computer network. Are apps made of services, being just thin
clients, gateways to the clouds? The truth is that some are, but far
from all. To understand apps, we need to realize they are actors
in a network that we will try to describe in the following.

Coordinating Sensors

Sweeping generalisations about apps are common, but an app can be most anything, from simple a utility to a complex game. Apple's App Store contains map applications, medical diagnostic tools, exercise journals, recipe books and diet journals, banking apps and bus ticket apps, unit converters, calculators and the simple flashlight. The only common aspect seems to be the device: Apps are software applications for mobile devices. Let us then begin the description of the app networks with the iPhone itself.

When the iPhone was introduced, Apple announced it as three new devices combined: An e-mail device, a music player, and a phone (Apple 2007). We may still tend to think of the iPhone as a remediation (Bolter and Grusin 1999) of the telephone, but the technical specification of an iPhone makes it very clear that it is much more. It is a pocket-sized computer with several network connections: GSM telephony, 801.11 Wi-fi, Bluetooth, USB, and in the 2014 models even Near-Field Communication (Apple 2014a).

Input can be given via the high-resolution touch screen, a microphone and camera on both the front and the back the phone, and a few buttons. Output is given through the screen, three loudspeakers, a vibrator, or a powerful LED light, and more loudspeakers and screens can be connected with wires. It is important not to forget the sensors: GPS, proximity sensor, barometer, an accelerometer, a three-way gyroscope for compass and movement, an ambient light sensor, and a fingerprint scanner in some models.

An iPhone app is a small program that uses some of these net-work connections, input/output and sensors for a purpose the user finds useful or entertaining. An app can make calculations, based on input from the user or the sensors, send and receive data over a network, and output the results to the user, and simultaneously send the results over a network. The most popular apps are in fact thin clients for Web services, such as Facebook and Google Maps. They use the network extensively, and most calculations are performed on the remote server, "in the cloud". But other popular apps, for example Angry Birds, perform calculations on the iPhone, and use the touch screen and the loudspeakers of the iPhone for interaction. Yet other apps rely on other sensors, such as Sleep Cycle which uses the accelerometer to monitor how the users move while sleeping, or VitalSigns which calculates the pulse and breathing rate of the person in front of the camera by analysing the image. The 2014 Apple Design Award winner Device 6 is an interactive story midway between a game and a book, using only the touch screen and the loudspeakers, while Flashlight uses only the touch screen to switch the LED flash on and off. Sleep Cycle, VitalSigns, Device 6, and Flashlight do not communicate with any server, they run in isolation on the iPhone.

To state that there is no software, only services, would be to narrow down this multitude to only a few kinds of apps. I find Liestøl's perspective more fruitful: That we are moving into the age of sensory media (Liestøl et al. 2012). I believe this transition needs to be studied extensively, but for this essay, we need to move on in our description of the network; from the apps running on the device to the app developers and the environment they work in.

Here be Software

Kittler received some attention for the provocative article title "There is no Software" (Kittler 1992), where he argues the many layers of computer software are only masking the underlying hardware of the computer. In all its technological determinism, the article is mainly a critique of modern computers' Cartesian foundation. Kittler could code in several programming languages, and knew very well that software is the quite tangible result of labour, often tremendous labour. Its layered structure makes this labour more efficient, and instead of analysing it away, a software studies approach should focus on these different layers, and see how power is distributed throughout.

One does not design an app by combining web services. Apps for iOS can only be made with Apple's XCode programming environment for Macintosh computers. It includes two languages and 70 different frameworks programmers can draw on, including interface buttons and other elements, cloud storage in Apple's server parks, a database system, graphics engines for 2D and 3D development, and interfaces to other parts of iOS, such as notifications, address book, calendar, maps, camera, and photo editing software. These frameworks are similar to services both in being standardised design patterns that developers can rely on through a relatively simple interface, and in being "black boxes", as developers do not need to understand their inner workings.

There are frameworks to support all the three main operations we outlined above; local calculations, access to the sensors , and access to Apple's cloud services. Programmers may earn money by using Apple's frameworks for purchases within the app through App Store's payment service, and for banner ads inside the app. Cloud storage in Apple's iCloud is available through another framework, and sharing via Facebook and Twitter is done via yet another.

XCode is a powerful actor in the network: It regulates what can be done, what is simple to do, and what simply can't be done, and thus has power over its developers. Zittrain uses the iPhone as a prime example of a "tethered" device that can be remotely controlled by its manufacturers, in opposition to a "generative" device that can be made to do anything (Zittrain 2008, chap. 2–3). This division is too simple. Apple can control some aspects of iPhones through software updates, and some of the frameworks and services that developers may use can be remotely controlled. Developers have still found the freedom to create 1.5 million apps available in the US store, which seems quite generative. Apple's frameworks rarely lock developers in, but they provide roads of less resistance. Large corporations like Facebook operate their own services that their apps use. Smaller developers will have to develop their own services, or they can take the simpler route and use Apple's. Rather than using a dichotomy of generative/tethered, we should follow Kittler's example (if not his conclusions) and study the degrees of freedom available through the software layers.

Software as a Service is often pictured as an architecture that makes programming simple. Apparently, developers do not need to code, just assemble different services, like a child connecting Lego bricks. Programming for iOS programming is a far way from this. Just to create the traditional beginners' "hello world" message requires a list of different files, most of which are unintelligible for a beginner. 500 million iPhones have been sold (Costello 2014), only 350 000 of the owners have registered as developers, and many of these developers (we do not know how many) have never uploaded an app to App Store. One could imagine a phone so easy to program that users would create a flashlight app, not download one, but the iPhone is not that product.

App Store: The Obligatory Passage Point

Just as XCode is the only programming environment, Apple has a monopoly on distribution; developers can't just send apps to their friends. To test a new app on an actual iPhone, the developer must purchase a $99 per year license from Apple (Apple 2014b). The app can be tested on a few devices only, and can only be distributed further via Apple's App Store. This is the main node in the iOS network we are describing, and what Callon (1986) would describe as an "obligatory passage point."

App Store contained close to 1.5 million apps at the end of 2014. It is a place for small businesses, as discussed by Snickars (2012) and Flueckiger (2012), although major services power the most popular apps (App Annie).

Apple reviews every app before it is allowed into the App Store, and the "App Store Review Guidelines" (Apple 2015) contain 179 rules. Apple controls that apps are reliable, safe, and consistent with the iPhone interface guidelines. Apple also protects its market position, and "apps or metadata that mentions the name of any other mobile platform will be rejected" (rule 3.1). Violence, racism, sex, medical advice and mentions of drug, alcohol, or nicotine use are all strictly governed. This has spurred a debate on censorship, as witnessed by the Wikipedia page "Censorship by Apple" (Wikipedia contributors 2015).

Apple collects a fee for every review. Approved apps can be distributed for free, or the developer can choose to sell it, in which case Apple keeps 30 percent of the revenue. To download an app, users must submit their private Apple ID and password, and charge paid apps to the credit card associated with the account.

Apple is by far the strongest power in these meetings with developers, software, registration fees and credit card companies, these "trials of strength" (Latour 1988). Developers also have power, however. The iPhone had not been the success it is without this tremendous creativity on the part of the developers, as Snickars (2012) has shown. Users on their side judge, one by one, which apps they want to install and use, which is no small power, as the competition for downloads is strong. When users choose which apps to keep, they arbitrate in the trials of strength between the other actors.

Mobility and Ubiquity: Clients and Clouds

We have drawn a quick sketch of the app network, indicating some power relations. We now can return to the question of SaaS. App development is not mashing up services by the inexperienced. Still, apps may connect to Facebook, Twitter, Google's many services, and personal storage clouds like Evernote or DropBox. This is *ubiquitous computing*: Your data is always with you; the clouds are always over your head. But the idea of the one thin client for all software is lost. Although the mobile phone is powerful it is too slow for the advanced client-side scripts that modern web services use. Mobile telephony networks are also much slower than broadband connections in desktop computers. Efficiency is a major reason to create an app rather than using the telephone's web browser. Apple's Objective-c is more efficient than JavaScript, and gives the developer more control over the many software frameworks and hardware sensors. Another reason is the tiny screen: The browser has a few lines of user interface (known as "chrome") that eat up precious space. Facebook on the Safari browser is shown with the address bar on top and the back button and other controls on the bottom. The Facebook app can use the whole screen, and is at the same time more efficient.

Cloud computing on the phone is not one, but many thin clients. Each of these must be installed and kept up to date, and while the App Store software can notice users of available updates, SaaS's main promise of no installs, no upgrades is lost.

Conclusion

Apps will not kill the Web. While there are some overlaps between web sites and apps, there is a considerable number of apps that never have been, and never will be web services. Anderson's point is that a lot of what is now available as commercial services on the web, such as news and social media, can be delivered more efficiently and reliably on apps tailor-made for each platform. It should not be a surprise that the media industry is what is most visible from Anderson's perspective as an editor of a print magazine. Amateur participation is for Zittrain and others the strength of the Web, and the one aspect that makes it a unique technology.

Amateurs make many apps, but most apps are probably made by professional programmers in their spare time. To create an app is to enter a network of, Apple's programming languages and the Xcode application, Apple's approval service, Apple's App Store, users, and the iPhone itself.

Apps are more than services, they are applications that put the iPhone's computing facilities, network connections, sensors and output devices to use for purposes that do not provoke Apple, and that users find meaningful.

I would like to thank Anders Sundnes Løvlie, Frode Guribye, Kjartan Michalsen, and Johannes M. Ringheim for insightful discussions. The Department of Media and Information Science, University of Bergen kindly lent me the office space where I wrote this text.

Bibliography

Anderson, Chris. 2010a. "The Web Is Dead? A Debate." *Wired,* September 17. Accessed December 19, 2014. http://www.wired.com/magazine/2010/08/ff_webrip_debate/.

Anderson, Chris. 2010b. "The Web is Dead: Long Live The Internet." *Wired,* September 17. Accessed May 27, 2015. http://www.wired.com/2010/08/ff_webrip.

App Annie. "iOS Top App Charts." Accessed April 14, 2015. https://www.appannie.com/apps/ios/top/?_ref=header&device=iphone.

Apple. 2007. "Apple Reinvents the Phone With the Iphone." *Apple Press Info*, January 9. Accessed December 19, 2014. https://www.apple.com/pr/library/2007/01/09-Apple-Reinvents-the-Phone-with-iPhone.html.

Apple. 2014a. "Iphone 6: Technical Specifications." *Apple iPhone.* Accessed December 19, 2014. http://www.apple.com/iphone-6/specs/.

Apple. 2014b. "iOS Developer Program." *Apple Developer.* Accessed December 19, 2014. https://developer.apple.com/programs/ios/.

Apple. 2015. "App Store Review Guidelines." *Apple Developer.* Accessed April 14, 2015. https://developer.apple.com/app-store/review/guidelines/.

Bolter, Jay David, and Richard Grusin. 1999. *Remediation: Understanding New Media.* Cambridge, MA: MIT Press.

Callon, Michel. 1986. "Some Elements of a Sociology of Translation: Domestication of the Scallops and the Fishermen of St Brieuc Bay." In *Power, Action and Belief: A New Sociology of Knowledge?,* edited by John Law, 196–223. London: Routledge.

Costello, Sam. 2014. "How Many Iphones Have Been Sold Worldwide?" *about tech.* Accessed December 19, 2014. http://ipod.about.com/od/glossary/f/how-many-iphones-sold.htm.

Flueckiger, Barbara. 2012. "The Iphone Apps: A Digital Culture of Interactivity." In *Moving Data: The Iphone and the Future of Media*, edited by Pelle Snickars and Patrick Vonderau, 171–183. New York: Columbia University Press.

Kittler, Friedrich. 1992. "There is no Software." *Stanford Literature Review* 9 (1): 81–90.

Latour, Bruno. 1988. *The Pasteurization of France*. Cambridge, MA: Harvard University Press.

Liestøl, Gunnar, Anne Doksrød, Šarunas Ledas, and Terje Rasmussen. 2012. "Sensory Media: Multidisciplinary Approaches in Designing a Situated & Mobile Learning Environment for Past Topics." *International Journal of Interactive Mobile Technologies* 6 (3): 24–28.

Snickars, Pelle. 2012. "A Walled Garden Turned Into a Rainforest." In *Moving Data: The Iphone and the Future of Media*, edited by Pelle Snickars, and Patrick Vonderau, New York, NY: Columbia University Press.

The Open Group. 2013. "Using TOGAF to Define and Govern SOAs: Service-Oriented Archtecture Defined." *The SOA Source Book*. Accessed May 27, 2015. https://www.opengroup.org/soa/source-book/togaf/soadef.htm.

Wikipedia contributors, "Censorship by Apple." *Wikipedia: The Free Encyclopedia.* Last modified February 22, 2015, 14:04 CET. Accessed April 14, 2015. http://en.wikipedia.org/w/index.php?title=Censorship_by_Apple&oldid=648325693.

Zittrain, Jonathan L. 2008. *The Future of the Internet and How to Stop it*. New Haven, CT: Yale University Press.

DDOS

COMPUTER VIRUS

INTERNET ECONOMY

SECURITY

NETWORK POLITICS

DOS

KIMDOTCOM

Denials of Service

Jussi Parikka

This article addresses denial-of-service attacks as one key entry point to understanding contemporary issues in network politics. By way of underlining the spiraling feature of the Internet economy as based on security and attack services, it leads into discussing the December 2014 DoS attack against Sony and Xbox gaming networks which were resolved by Kimdotcom offering the hackers vouchers for his file-sharing service, Mega. The article considers the implications of this and other examples in the context of how service has also come to denote a relationship to Internet infrastructure: Servers and the speed of Internet connections that can be slowed down or flooded by way of denial-of-service attacks.

Assumed Service

Service can be considered a general term that designates one major axis of network politics. Software is a service on so many levels. It is, after all, under the rubric of service that one enters into platforms and their terms of use; is granted or denied access to content such as newspapers, media or other things behind a paywall; gets connected on social networks such as gaming network and other forms of fun that, too, are a service. As by the end of this short text becomes clear, *denial-of-services* (DoS) are also services—and they can also be tackled with the further provision of service vouchers. The software-based economy is one of competing services whether we are talking of the official platforms such as social media or the more informal, sometimes criminal, services such as DoS.

Service also implies key cognitive and social skills as the site of extracting value and monetisation. It is, after all, in the service economy that services are effectively invented as ways of accessing your needs, relations and other forms in which value might be discovered. The social is not merely about the factory, as we learned in the post-Fordist political theory; the social is also a service as long as one is able to package it as such. In other words, in the contemporary social media and service economy, the social is accessed as a service.

Besides being a nexus of such relations, where the social and the economic conflate, one can approach service through another link. In terms of technological culture and technological (media) systems, one can follow in the footsteps of Paul Virilio and Wolfgang Schivelbusch in starting to track the nature of technological systems through their breaking points. With the invention of the train comes the train wreck, the history of aviation is one of a systematic relation to the air craft accidents and similarly across a range of technological inventions, one can write the history of their specific accidents. One can write the media archaeology of technology through its breaking points and analyze how, for example, computers, software and networks such as the Internet, look if one starts from their specific forms of accidents. One can claim that computer worms and viruses have been one such central form of an accident that unfolds the wider logic and implicit infrastructural desires of network culture in relation to universal communicability, exchange and sharing (Parikka 2007; Cohen 1986). This suggests that one can also address the issue of services from the perspective of denial-of service attacks, one recurring/repetitive form of software-based practice that has been coined both as a new form of new political activism and as much as harmful hacking.

Through DoS activities, the idea of services as the mask of software becomes one related to security and commerce. In short, denial-of-service attacks have become part of the vocabulary of media reports and security evaluation of Internet culture since the latter half of the 1990s. In simple, rather non-technical terms, denial-of-service attacks work by bombarding a specific address and its server. The Internet economy of "pings" and "hits" is turned against itself by a technically-induced surge in "popularity" over a short period of time, causing the server to crash and become unavailable. The whole attack has a curious relation to the time of the Internet "pings" (see Pias 2011) and the time-critical infrastructure of the Internet (Ernst 2013) in terms of producing a request time out; or in other words, producing a situation of technical inability to handle requests (being flooded, a situation of service desk management under extreme customer inflow, so to speak). Situations of bureaucracy and customer service turn into problems of Internet traffic and its protocological management, just like social situations of services and servantry have turned into both symbolic signs and cultural techniques of the software search economy (Krajewski 2010). Software turns around the axis of service, whether providing or denying service.

Cultural Techniques of Denial

As writers such as Finn Brunton (2013) have explained, DoS
or *distributed-denial-of service* (DDoS) attacks using botnets,
are a feature of the history of malicious software. As early as
the late 1980s and early 1990s, dangers of worms and viruses
were identified in the context of commercial transactions,
communication and services. Security measures extended
to insurance with Lloyds of London in 1989 already offering
packages for network-related incidents. The policy was to cover
against loss of telecommunications, software and data faults,
as well as virus attacks. Around the same period, Control Risks
Group Ltd. formed a new company called Control Risks Information Technology Ltd. (CRIT), which was tasked with combatting
computer crime, including espionage, fraud, malicious or illegal
data modification, and denial- or destruction-of-services (Parikka
2007, 73). In the unending spiral of the service economy, this situation refers to a service to cover against loss of service.

Worms such as Mydoom (2004) and many others have become
milestones in this alternative history of the Internet service
economy (read through its underbelly). However, the various
cultural techniques of actually denying a service, are even
more abundant, including smurfing and fraggling as ways to
enforce bandwidth consumption, ICMP (*Internet Control Message
Protocol*) echo request/reply pinging, and even by sending single
malicious packets such as the Invite of Death attacks using the
Internet telephony protocol (VoIP). Such techniques relate to the
protocological nature of the Internet (Galloway 2004) but also
open up as specific ways of emphasizing the issue of service over
software. Of course, when it comes to issues of service and their
denials, through a DoS perspective one starts to appreciate how
even zombie networks of bots are part and parcel in the for-
mation of the service relations of Internet platforms. A thousand
captured machines pinging your favorite games service network
is the call of the half-dead slowing down your bandwidth.

This primacy of service and its denial is an interesting feature in terms of software-related techniques. Indeed, it is one way of beginning the task of unfolding the peculiar emphasis on Internet sociability as one of relations of service. For there to be denial-of-service, an assumption of service has to be established as one prime feature of the social digital networks and its platforms. The discourse of services is actually a way of starting to consider whether, instead of software, the issues highlighted and at the centre of this sort of Internet "politics" are ones of servers, not software; of data traffic and speeds, not programs? Naturally one should not consider these things as binary opposites, but when referring to software politics, software studies, and other related terms, one has to remember that not all of the software focus refers back to end user programs, but the wider infrastructural questions and their service relations which sustain the specific modes of subjectivity in network economies: servers, servants, services and their customers (see Krajewski 2010 and 2013 for a thorough media history of servantry).

It is in this context, that the relation of service to "network politics" is emphasized with a twist. The service-induced bracketing of software—there is no software, only services—is a feature that can be addressed by way of analyzing the logic of DoS and service as a feature negotiated as part of Internet infrastructure: servers, bandwidth, slowness and speeds of pings, etc. Services offer access to content, but are also underpinned by how such content and the affective/cognitive economy is reliant on infrastructure. Over the past years, issues of *net neutrality* have dictated a major chunk of the debate on network politics: who is allowed to dictate Internet speeds, potential offering a fast lane to the best paying services over less wealthy users?

DoS offers a further commentary as to the speed and slowness as services. One can even buy this slowing down as a service by way of hiring suitable hacker groups (Brunton 2013; Dredge 2014), just like one is offered services of "neighborhood watch" of distributed webmasters, data management and distributed clouds to ensure the accessibility of your site even for individuals or small groups/companies (e. g. CloudFlare 2015). Security services extend from mere protection against malicious software to encompass visitor management, content distribution across servers, and traffic optimization.

In any case, all of this illuminates the various levels at which service operates from the service one buys and assumes in terms of content, feeling, user satisfaction and such end-user customer contexts, but also the infrastructural level involved in a network relation: for example, the assumed speed.

Voucher Solutions

As an example of the curious twists of the discourse of service and denial-of-service in Internet culture, consider this example from the end of 2014. During the Christmas holidays in 2014, on Boxing Day, the hacker group Lizard Squad claimed responsibility for a denial-of-service attack on the Sony Playstation and Xbox networks. In the middle of the post-Christmas gaming frenzy, the attack brought down the networks, making headlines as the hacking incidents had done earlier in December. The alleged North Korean hacking of Sony reached an odd consumer-centred "political" debate about censorship as it looked like Sony would pull its film *The Interview* from distribution. Of course, the Sony hack by the group Guardians of Peace focused primarily on capturing a wealth of material from Sony and was different to the Lizard Squad attack.

In a manner that also provides a curious commentary on the notion of network politics, the Lizard Squad situation was resolved by a very surprising mediator, Kimdotcom, the controversial founder of Megaupload, the Mega storage/sharing service and a vocal Internet rights and freedoms activist. According to his own testimony, the hackers were offered vouchers for premium Mega Lifetime accounts in exchange for ending the attack and promising never to do it again.

The situation was resolved with both sides releasing Twitter statements.

Lizard Squad (@lizardmafia) commented in a very satisfied tone: "Thanks @KimDotcom for the vouchers--you're the reason we stopped the attacks. @MegaPrivacy is an awesome service."

The happy tone was echoed by Kimdotcom on Twitter: "Xbox Live and PSN services coming back. Many regions fully restored. Full recovery imminent. Enjoy your gaming holidays. You're welcome :-)"

Later on the same day, December 26, 2014, "Remember... Lizard Squad only gets the benefit of free Mega premium accounts if they don't attack Xbox Live & PSN again. #Thatsthedeal".

This did not, however, stop Lizard Squad from offering their services as a separate DDoS-tool called the LizardStresser that one could hire for Internet attack needs: "LizardStresser's highest level of attack promises 30,000 seconds—just over eight hours— for $129.99 a month or $500 for for 'lifetime' usage" (Dredge 2014).

Besides DDoS as a service, the case of the Mega storage/sharing platform is also a curious commentary on the Internet economy. As part of the new vanguard of Internet hero sort of politics of individual cult-producing freedom fighters (alongside, for example, Julian Assange) Kimdotcom's politics-accused-of-piracy has turned to quoting the *Universal Declaration of Human Rights* on the home page of the storage/sharing platform Mega, branded as

The Privacy Company: No one shall be subjected to arbitrary interference with his privacy, family, home or correspondence. Everyone has the right to the protection of law against such interference. (Mega 2015a)

Storage and privacy become part and parcel of their business, or more specifically, as specified in Mega's Terms of Service:

Our service includes UCE [user controlled encryption]. You should keep your encryption keys safe and confidential and not release them to anyone unless you wish them to have access to your data. If you lose or misplace your encryption keys, you will lose access to your data. We strongly urge you to use robust anti-virus and firewall protection. (Mega 2015b)

Significantly, as hacking and related techniques have been adopted as part of the discourse of network politics over the past years, it can also refer to a service-oriented "politics" or "diplomacy" that counters denials-of-service with access to service. Kimdotcom's offer (#thatsthedeal), counters the hacker actions by a Christmas gift of free encrypted storage vouchers ensuring access to gaming network services for millions of users. The culture of vouchers, from shopping and even the privatization of service economies in the wake of austerity policies, signify the ability to choose to be cherished by neoliberal discourse.

Anyhow, in our case, it marks a variation of "there is no software, there are just services" to "there is no software, just vouchers"—a quasi-political service-oriented solution to problems of denials-of-service.

Many thanks to Geraldine Juárez for her feedback and ideas.

Bibliography

Brunton, Finn. 2013. *Spam. A Shadow History of the Internet*. Cambridge, MA: MIT Press.

Cohen, Frederick B. 1986. *Computer Viruses*. A Dissertation presented at the University of Southern California, December.

CloudFlare. 2015. "Give us five minutes and we'll supercharge your website." *CloudFlare, Inc.* Accessed May 28, 2015. https://www.cloudflare.com/.

Dredge, Stuart. 2014. "Lizardsquad now helping anyone copy its Playstation and Xbox attacks." *The Guardian*, December 31. Accessed May

28, 2015. http://www.theguardian.com/technology/2014/dec/31/ **111**
lizard-squad-ddos-service-playstation-xbox-lizardstresser.

Krajewski, Markus. 2010. "Ask Jeeves. Servants as Search Engines." *Grey Room* 38
(Winter): 6–19.

Krajewski, Markus. 2013. "The power of small gestures: On the cultural
technique of service." *Theory, Culture & Society* 30 (6): 94–109.

Mega. 2015a. "Info." *MEGA: The Privacy Company.* Accessed May 28, 2015. https://
mega.co.nz/#info.

Mega. 2015b. "Terms of Service." *MEGA: The Privacy Company.* Accessen May 28, 2015.
https://mega.co.nz/#terms.

Parikka, Jussi 2007. *Digital Contagions. A Media Archaeology of Computer Viruses.* New
York: Peter Lang.

Pias, Claus 2011. "The Game Player's Duty. The User as the Gestalt of the Ports."
In: *Media Archaeology. Approaches, Applications and Implications*, edited by Erkki
Huhtamo and Jussi Parikka, 163–183. Berkeley: University of California Press.

Authors

Seth Erickson is a PhD candidate at the Department of Information Studies, University of California, Los Angeles. His dissertation focuses on software development practices in contemporary digital scholarship.

Anders Fagerjord is Associate Professor of Media Studies at the Department of Media and Communication, University of Oslo. His research interests include locative media, design theory, multimodality and multimedia theory; and the concept of "convergence." Outside of academia, he has worked as a web designer and radio host.

Irina Kaldrack is a Postdoctoral Researcher at the Digital Cultures Research Lab, Leuphana University of Lüneburg. Her work concerns new methods in the digital age, the theory and history of digital cultures, the scientific history of motion, and the cultural history of mathematics.

Christopher M. Kelty is Professor of Information Studies and Anthropology at the University of California, Los Angeles. He is the author of *Two Bits: The Cultural Significance of Free Software*. Current research projects can be found at http://kelty.org/.

Martina Leeker is Professor of Methods in Digital Cultures and Senior Researcher at the Digital Cultures Research Lab, Leuphana University of Lüneburg. She is a scholar and lecturer for theater and media studies. Her research concerns artistic/practical research in digital cultures, discourse-analytical media theory, media-anthropology, art and technology, theater and media.

Andrew Lison is a Postdoctoral Researcher in the Digital Humanities at the Hall Center for the Humanities, University of Kansas. He is co-editor, with Timothy Scott Brown, of *The Global Sixties in Sound and Vision: Media, Counterculture, Revolt* (Palgrave Macmillan, 2014). His work has also appeared in *New Formations* and *Science Fiction Studies*.

114   **Liam Magee** is a Senior Research Fellow at the Institute for Culture and Society, University of Western Sydney. He is co-author of *Towards a Semantic Web: Connecting Knowledge in Academic Research* (2010).

Christoph Neubert is a Postdoctoral Lecturer for Media History at the Department of Media Studies, University of Paderborn and senior member of the DFG Research Training Group "Automatisms." His research interests include media theory and history, the epistemology of traffic and logistics, and the history of ecology.

Jussi Parikka is Professor of Technological Culture & Aesthetics at Winchester School of Art, University of Southampton. He is the author of several books on digital culture and media theory, including *What is Media Archaeology?* (2012) and most recently *A Geology of Media* (2015).

Ned Rossiter is Professor of Communication at the Institute for Culture and Society, University of Western Sydney. His book *Software, Infrastructure, Labor: A Media Theory of Logistical Nightmares* is forthcoming in 2015.